C000256470

PEAK LIFE'S WORK

FIND YOUR GIFT AND GIVE IT AWAY

PEAK PRODUCTIVITY
BOOK 5

SAID HASYIM

Edited by
DAVID ARETHA, ANDREA VANRYKEN

For Lin Lin Aung

Who remains unbreakable no matter what life throws at her.

Just like a bamboo that thrives in the harshest conditions, yet its roots burrow deep into the earth.

Life is too short to waste dreaming of someone else's passion. Create yours.

CONTENTS

PREFACE

After wandering from one thinking nook to another for six years, I finally completed the manuscript of this book.

As I wrote the last section of this book in the solitude of early hours in a park, I pondered what it was going to take for me to not publish this book.

While the sun warmed my right cheek, and five ducklings sauntered the green, lush grass, I realized how fortunate I have been to be afforded the chance and time to finish this book. Who am I not to share this piece of knowledge with the world?

If I can change a person's life for the better, I'll take the chance on doing so. It is my honor to present you with this book.

INTRODUCTION

Once upon a time, you had a dream to start your own business, act on stage, or even become a rap star. That fantasy lingered in your mind for a long time, until one day your friend told you it was impossible, your sibling said, "Keep dreaming," or your coach remarked, "I don't mean to hurt you, but that is farfetched."

Your desire to fulfill your dream was shattered that day. What everyone said sounded true, and you needed to return to reality. You were not that talented anyway. Life goes on. You remained mired in the same slough.

You continued to work hard your entire life, aiming at only one goal: to earn a lot of money to retire comfortably. When you finally had enough money to retire, you realized that the sudden extra free time left you bored. When you do not know how to spend your time, you will resort to killing your time. That's a sad reality that many cannot admit.

If you can't wait to retire, you have not been living your life fully. You have not been taking pleasure in what you do. That's why when you are granted that enormous amount of free time, you don't know how to use it productively.

If we never pursue our potential in life, we will leave nothing in this world that can be of service to our children or to humanity as a whole; no inventions or great ideas. We will do nothing other than consume what others offer.

Discovering your gift gives meaning to life. Without knowing your gift, you are swayed by your environment. Your talent remains latent and is never used to fill up your void. You live in the hollowness of the world, like society expects you to do.

Honing your gifts to create your life's work and then later giving it away by making it accessible for the betterment of humanity gives you a purpose. Everyone is born with a set of unique abilities meant to contribute to the world's furtherance. The world needs our temporary existence to furnish it with creations assembled through the gifts bestowed to all of us.

This book chronicles the findings and lessons that I have spent more than a decade working on, satiating my incessant desire to find my gift and use it to create a fulfilled life. I finally discovered my gift with certainty at thirty-one and never looked back. My life has been a genuine pleasure every day. Improving my innate strengths has been my source of enjoyment. Since then, all the life decisions I have made have been based on whether I can advance my gifts. After saving enough to carry out my life's task, I surrendered my day job.

I have been living an uncertain and yet rewarding life. Every day is a new discovery. I can't wait to get off my bed every morning to do the work I *want* to do while at the same time, honing my skills. Six years into my life's task, the dividends have paid off in life satisfaction many times over.

Your gift can be a dominant source of galvanic motivation, inspiration, and creativity. If you haven't explored your gift yet, it's time to start. What is confined in you that can serve humanity? Through this book, we will unearth your heart's desire, maximize your strengths, and prepare you to create a life's work that only you can do.

1

THE GIFT

> A wonderful gift may not be wrapped as you expect.
>
> — JONATHAN LOCKWOOD HUIE

THE *GIFT* IS A TERM THAT REFERS TO AN INVISIBLE, INTANGIBLE quality or attribute of a person. I refer to it as a person's innate talents, interests, character strengths, and relevant skills.

Everyone is born with some innate gifts. If you draw better than most people, you have a better chance of becoming a successful artist. Unfortunately, not everyone knows what gift they own. Maybe you've been told you should be a writer or an artist but weren't sure if it was just a passing fancy.

If you already know exactly what your talent is, you will be lucky enough to get to know your true self. For many of us, finding our innate talent is a long, hard, and sometimes painful process. A few have been told consistently that they possess certain desirable abilities, whereas most people's latent talents remain undiscovered. If you are an adult reading this book now, you must have developed something within you that is just waiting to be found—if you haven't found it already.

The Four Pillars

There are four components that constitute a gift:

- **Character strengths** are the traits that are generally regarded as desirable by many cultures, such as love of learning, honesty, and discipline. These are what make your personality shine.
- **Talent** is ears for music, eyes for details, or a nose for business. Talent is foremost in your genes. It is fixed for you.
- **Interest** is what draws you back to something again and again; for example, interest in empathizing with animals, playing table tennis, or drawing people.
- **Skill** is what you gain while navigating the challenges of life such as making a fire, riding a bicycle, or knitting clothes.

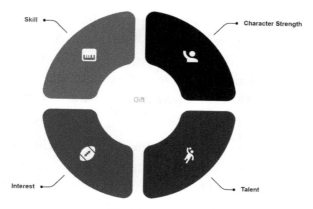

The Gift Components

It is important to differentiate between each of these four components in your quest to discover your true gift. The overly simplified advice, "Follow your passion," can quickly set you up for a lifetime of disappointment. You may be interested in swimming, but it might not be your talent. Without much deliberation, you may live your life thinking that you have a talent for swimming, only to end up disappointed that you haven't achieved much of a swimming career. You may think you have a talent for playing chess when your actual talent is strategic thinking. Or maybe you have no talent for playing chess at all but you have developed an interest in that game and have the skills to play it well.

You use the confluence of these four pillars to pursue your life's work. Knowing what you possess makes it easier for you to define what you want to do.

Hone Your Gift

Being born with a gift is not a guarantee that you will be successful in your life. You can't achieve your goal without growing into the person who can. Once you discover your true abilities, you can then hone them for life. Make a plan to upgrade them. Figure out what you can do with these skills. Don't let them wither because you rarely tap them in your current job or activities. These abilities can alter your life for the better. Use them to synergize with what you are already doing to produce novel perspectives.

Nurture your gifts to the maximum of their capacities, even if it means going through years or decades of apprenticeships. You will reap the reward of high satisfaction. The world needs us— people with diverse innate abilities who are willing to make a concerted effort to bloom and produce something that benefits the masses and creates posterity.

When you develop your gift every day, you trigger positive changes in your brain. The more you use your gift, the better your brain gets at using it. The brain's ability to adapt and change in response to your experiences is known as neuroplasticity. You can read more about neuroplasticity in the third book of this series, *Peak Brain Plasticity*. As much as possible, venture into using your gift at every opportunity. Remember that you are already in a more favorable position to use these gifts than most people. Your gift is your unique, unfair advantage.

The convergence of your innate abilities and the opportunities that present themselves to you results in something unique for you to do and do well. People often take the path of least resistance because they are unsure of what else to try. However, with some effort, it is possible to uncover your gift and find the path that will lead you to fulfillment.

Barriers to Maximizing Your Gifts

Had Jimmy Fallon succeeded in major films auditions, he may not have climbed to the top of the late-night show ladder in such a short time. If Soichiro Honda had been successful in his job as an engineer, he may never have undertaken the tasks that ultimately inspired him to make his own scooters and develop Honda Motor Company.

A wrong choice—that may seem good at the onset—could set you back years in reaching your goals. But with the right one—even if it does not seem profitable—and some luck, you can be quickly propelled toward your goal.

Life is full of randomness. If you are going by all your apparently excellent options, it might seem incredibly difficult to successfully forecast which choice will lead to success the quickest.

The common factors that can keep you from developing your gifts are:

1. Your job

YOUR VOCATION, if chosen correctly, can propel you toward your end goal. Most often, when we enter the workforce, we don't give enough thought to anything other than whether the job matches the degree we graduated with. Fair enough—we are all young and naïve at that point.

At our job, let's say we were all quite successful, and the pay was rather decent, even though the work felt like a drag. Every day, we looked forward to the weekend. As we climbed the corporate ladder, we secured a position that had little to no relevance to our gift. Since the pay was good, we became very comfortable with the job. We stopped improving but still went to work just so we could draw the salary.

At the time, we knew for sure that we didn't like our job, but when it grew too comfortable for us, our inner talent was buried deeper. We may think that our calling was to do that job, but it is just that your colleagues became too reliant on you. Watch out for jobs that drain your soul, no matter how adept you are at them.

2. Monetary rewards

WE MAY SELECT a college degree that potentially grants us access to a high-paying job. We may choose a vocation that will pay the most regardless of our natural inclinations. Because society largely considers money the metric of success, you may feel drawn to what will earn you the most attractive wages.

As long as you earn reasonably well, you may be hesitant to move around. Starting your own uncertain venture might be the farthest thing from your mind. You might still focus on that venture but just as a hobby. A hobby remains a hobby if you can't blossom it into a full-scale realization that can be subjected to public criticism and that generates genuine feedback to grow you. A hobby limits the time you can spend practicing and improving. As a result, you drift farther away from your dream.

Creative work is always uncertain. If you must have assurance that your venture will guarantee a lot of money, you will likely never start your life's work. You will never hone your true abilities.

Wolfgang Amadeus Mozart would have stuck to composing European music if he had wanted financial security. Instead, he went on to compose opera-style music, which was risky and not well-received in his time. That controversial music genre later became one of the most world-renowned in the world.

3. People's expectations

OUR PARENTS MAY INCESSANTLY EXPECT us to learn and succeed in their business or enroll in the most prestigious university for a better chance of joining the highest pecking order in society. Because we spend most of our time with our parents, they hold a tremendous influence over us.[1] We depend on them during our youth. They can repress our dream by insisting we take piano lessons instead of drawing or study literature instead of exploring various species outdoors.

As we grow older, we notice that our parents' expectations align with the majority of society's: Graduate top in the class, get a good job, buy a big house, get married, and raise children. We've confused those expectations with our desires. This situation further re-enacts our parents' tenet and inhibits what we yearn for the most from our life.

OVERCOMING a problem requires having an awareness of what engenders it. Watch out for traps as you navigate through the ebb and flow of life's circumstances—which can masquerade as blessings.

The Pitfalls of Assessment Tools

Having a gift that stands out makes it easy to take notice of yourself, if not be noticed by others as well. If you are highly skillful at photography, for example, others can't help but take note of and appreciate what you can do.

But not everyone has gifts that are easily spotted. For good reason, many tools were invented to help people discover and gain clarity about their gifts. Many people use assessment tools such as the Myers–Briggs Type Indicator, StrengthsFinder 2.0, or the Enneagram test to realize their gift. Each of these tests measures different aspects of a person's personality. This information can then be used to help people find their interest.

While these can be helpful in giving you some insight into your strengths to some extent, they have some limitations that could mislead you:

1. Potentially inaccurate results

QUESTION-BASED assessment tools often ask you to rate your interest in different topics or activities. However, rating your interest can be misleading because it does not reflect how passionate you are about it. Your interest is measured rather than your abilities. Someone who reports being an intuitive thinker may actually be better at problem-solving through deduction than through intuition because their interest lies in problem-solving rather than in intuition per se.

Additionally, some assessments require you to input your answers within a certain time period, which opens up more room for error because the correctness of your answers would then depend on:

- Your mood at that time
- The accuracy of your interpretation of the questions
- The pressure of picking the answer fast

2. Limited assessed strengths

THE TOOL WAS CREATED to find a person's strength in a simple, quick, and easy way. However, it is important to note that human uniqueness is incredibly diverse. Each tool only assesses a number of different personal strengths. This limitation could lead to a limited understanding of your overall strengths and potential areas for growth.

There is just no way to get to the heart of the matter by answering the provided ninety-six questions. At best, it can only offer you a glimpse into the obvious strengths a person has from their list of common human personality traits—a list that isn't fully comprehensive. Sending you the incorrect result would spell disaster in your path toward finding your true gifts.

3. False belief

WHILE SOME PEOPLE may have great success using these assessment tools, these tools are just assessment programs written with some level of pre-defined logic to determine a list of configured traits based on your answers. The accuracy hinges on the underlying codes being error-free and on the right context from your answers, failing which would generate invalid results.

Furthermore, if you allow yourself to believe the invalid result, you will limit your ability to explore what you truly enjoy and could be good at. The true value of a discovery process comes when you allow yourself to be open to new opportunities and possibilities. Believing invalid results produced by such assessment tools might keep you stuck in your current path and prevent you from reaching your full potential.

———

THERE IS no one definitive way (including even the responses produced by such tools) to uncover your gift. The best way to discover it is through experimentation and personal exploration. Only *you* can find out what you have inside of you.

WE WILL COVER each gift component in the following chapters of this book and how to find them. By the end of each chapter, you will have a better understanding of what your gift components are and how to use them. We will start with character strengths.

2

CHARACTER STRENGTHS

 It is better to be alone than to be in bad company.

— GEORGE WASHINGTON

CHARACTER STRENGTHS ARE INTERNALLY DRIVEN AND ENDURING personal qualities that help us build upon our natural gifts. Strong character is an essential part of healthy life. Character strengths develop over time through experience with activities that require effort, thought, and concentration, all of which eventually become a part of our daily routine. Being aware of character strengths helps individuals focus on developing these strengths in their everyday life.

The Six Virtues

American psychologists Martin Seligman and Christopher Peterson divided twenty-four character traits into six virtues:

wisdom, courage, humanity, justice, temperance, and transcendence.[1]

- Wisdom: being able to see the big picture and understand complex concepts
- Courage: having the strength to face challenges and rise to the occasion
- Humanity: having a sense of compassion and caring for others
- Justice: being fair and treating others the way you want to be treated
- Temperance: maintaining a balanced perspective in all situations
- Transcendence: being able to see things from a higher perspective and looking at the bigger picture

These virtues make up your ability to cultivate your character to become a better person. Anyone can become successful if they have a strong sense of these six virtues.

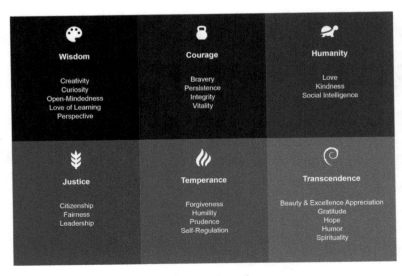

24 Character Strengths

Wisdom Virtue

Wisdom is the ability to discern the nature of things, to see beyond the apparent and understand the underlying principles. It involves being able to think critically and rationally about complex problems and issues and having a deep understanding of oneself and one's surroundings.

One of the most important things you can do for your own growth is to learn how to think critically. This involves understanding different perspectives, looking at data objectively, and solving problems using logic rather than sentiment or emotion. Wise people can see beyond their own experiences and perspectives to see the world as it is.

Martin Seligman and Christopher Peterson believe that wisdom is the key virtue for a successful life. They argue that people who are wise are better able to balance their emotions, think objectively, and make sound decisions. These abilities help them thrive in both personal and professional settings.

Courage Virtue

COURAGE IS the ability to be fearless in the face of danger or uncertainty. People who are brave stand up for what they believe in, even when it might be scary or difficult. They aren't afraid to take risks, and they don't shy away from tough challenges. This strength can be very useful in situations where there is a lot of pressure or chaos. It can also help you remain calm under pressure and when things get tough.

People who have courage will take risks even when they might be afraid. They have the strength of conviction to carry them through even the toughest challenges. This quality is essential in both a person's personal and professional life. People with courage can often be counted on when things get tough, no matter what the circumstances may be.

To have a strong sense of courage, it is important that you have a deep understanding of yourself and your capabilities. You need to be confident in your own abilities and know what you are willing to face to achieve your goals.

Humanity Virtue

THE HUMANITY VIRTUE is the ability to care about others. It encompasses compassion, understanding, and generosity. This ability goes beyond simply feeling empathy for others or committing to helping them; it is a deep-seated disposition that leads people to put themselves in others' shoes, see the world through their eyes, and act on behalf of others, expecting nothing in return.

People with a strong humanity virtue are good at empathizing with others and accepting them for who they are. These qualities make them good friends, allies, and advocates for social justice.

This is not a superficial or transient concern; rather, it is an enduring commitment that manifests itself in a host of ways. People who embody the virtue of humanity are often thoughtful and deliberate in their thoughts and actions, always looking out for the best interests of those around them. They are considerate and have strong moral convictions, which they put into practice by working on behalf of marginalized groups or advocating for social justice. In short, people who embody the virtue of humanity are kind-hearted individuals who put others first.

Justice Virtue

JUSTICE REFERS to our ability to live in accordance with the law and to treat people fairly, irrespective of their social or economic status. It also refers to our concern for the welfare of others. Justice requires understanding and empathy, as well as courage and strength. It is important to be fair and impartial, even when it might be difficult.

People who are good at justice can think critically and solve problems. They are also sympathetic and understanding. These qualities make them good leaders and allies as well as friends. They often have a strong sense of duty and set priorities wisely.

People who are bad at justice often find themselves in legal trouble or conflict with others. They may be unable to solve problems or manage their own emotions effectively. These qualities can make them unpopular leaders or partners and can lead them into conflicts that they cannot win.

Temperance Virtue

THE VIRTUE of temperance is the ability to control one's impulses and maintain a healthy balance in one's life. People who are temperate can delay gratification, resist temptations, and stay disciplined. They also have strong self-control, which makes them able to resist cravings and stay on track.

People who have strong temperance character also tend to be successful in other areas of their lives. Being able to control their emotions and impulses makes them less likely to act impulsively or out of anger. They can also maintain better boundaries with others, leading to healthier relationships overall. They are typically able to keep themselves organized and manage their time well, which can lead to success in life.

People who are lacking in temperance often resort to harmful behaviors, such as drinking or gambling excessively, in order to cope with stress. People with strong temperaments can keep their emotions in check even under pressure, which makes them supremely confident and resilient.

Transcendence Virtue

TRANSCENDENCE IS the ability to see things from a higher perspective. It entails being able to look at your own life and struggles from a larger perspective, seeing the world in all its beauty and complexity rather than just focusing on the individual details. This can be difficult to do, but it's an important quality for living a fulfilling life.

One way to cultivate transcendence is by learning about different cultures and religions. By understanding other people's beliefs, you'll come to see the world in a more holistic way and be better equipped to handle difficult situations. It also helps if you have empathy for other people, which allows you to put yourself in their shoes and understand their perspectives.

Another way to cultivate transcendence is through self-awareness. By constantly reflecting on your own thoughts and feelings, you'll become more aware of your own innermost desires and motivations. This can help you make better decisions based on what's truly important to you instead of succumbing to peer pressure or other external factors.

Intensity of the Strengths

Your character strengths serve as a foundation for how you will lead your life. Foul character can stop you from developing your talent or learning new skills, while moral character will help you move forward. If you are *dishonest*, you rarely fare well in your careers or relationships due to the lack of trust that develops over time. If you have high *curiosity*, you will likely build up a lot of knowledge. High *self-control* helps you combat procrastination in developing your talent. High *persistence* helps you learn tough skills.

You may occupy a lot or all of the twenty-four strengths, each with varying degrees of intensity. You may have a few very strong strengths that dominate your trait, or you may have many weak ones, but none of us possess all these twenty-four strengths with very high intensity. As a matter of fact, people who display ostensibly good character strengths may be fraudulent.

It is entirely possible that you are very weak in any of these strengths while having some very strong ones. An example would be a person with a high *love of learning* but very low *prudence*, such as twenty-two-year-old Eric Barcia, who was curious about bungee jumping and decided to conduct a bungee jump himself. Grabbing hold of the rope and tying it to the bridge, he leaped off the bridge after confirming that he'd carefully measured the bungee's length. What he failed to measure was the bungee cord's elasticity, which led to his premature death. It will behoove you to develop a good amount of all these character strengths, instead of only one, to succeed in life.

It is important to note that no matter how virtuous your traits are, you should be able to repress them based on some circumstances. You may even deliberately suppress your strengths in certain circumstances. At a funeral, for example, you may conceal your *humorous* character out of respect for others. At the office, you may avoid divulging your *perspective* to your superiors if you don't want to offend them.

In a similar vein, you need to be flexible in using the opposite strength to suit your situation. For example, there is no room to accede to false *hope* when you are not confronting the impeding problem. You may express anger (the opposite of *kindness*) to deal with an oppressor.

While these strengths do not change with technological progress, it is important to recognize that it is not impossible to change one's character traits. Research shows that we alter our character strengths from year to year.[2] Our strengths may change after some revelations. For example, we may become more confident because we can make it through whatever life throws at us. Or we may lose confidence in our ability to do so.

Strength Development

All these character strengths are not acquired in life simultaneously. The development of a certain strength begins at a certain stage of our life as we mature.[3]

Erik Erikson, an ego psychologist, developed the psychosocial theory of the development cycle.[4]

Psychosocial Crisis	Strength
Age 0 - 1	Trust vs Mistrust	Hope, Gratitude
Age 1 - 3	Autonomy vs Shame	Self-Regulation
Age 3 - 6	Initiative vs Guilt	Curiosity
Age 6 - 11	Industry vs Inferiority	Love of Learning, Creativity
Age 11 - 18	Identity vs Role Confusion	Social Intelligence, Spirituality
Age 18 - 25	Intimacy vs Isolation	Love
Age 25 - 50	Generativity vs Stagnation	Kindness
Age 50 - Death	Integrity vs Despair	Perspective

Erikson's Theory of Human Development

Birth to Age 1

An infant highly depends on the love of caregivers for survival. With reliable caregivers, the child develops trust and acquires *hope* and *gratitude*.

Inconsistent caregivers who are not always available for the infants breed mistrust. The problem is exacerbated when the parents lack affection and are emotionally unstable. The child will then develop a sense of fear that the world is unsafe.

Age 1 to 3

YOUNG CHILDREN MUST HAVE the freedom to exercise their will as they begin to gain a little independence. Granting them a greater sense of personal control gives them the autonomy to make things happen. It gives them *self-regulation*.

Children who are shamed for their struggles experience self-doubt and shame. They develop a sense of inadequacy.

Age 3 to 6

AT PRESCHOOL AGE, children begin to assert control over their environment. They take initiative to direct their play and lead social interactions, thus gaining the *curiosity* character strength.

If they fail to exercise initiative because of others' disapproval, they will develop a sense of guilt.

Age 6 to 11

IN SCHOOL, children begin to learn their abilities through learning and social interactions. If they succeed in overcoming the academic demands placed on them, their competence increases, and they gain *love of learning* and *creativity*.

Those who cannot cope with the school system and receive little encouragement from parents or teachers feel inferior.

Age 11 to 18

DURING THIS TURBULENT age of puberty, teenagers want to build their identity. They explore personal values they want to live by, gaining them *social intelligence* and *spirituality*.

Adolescents who cannot find an identity to represent themselves are left with confusion and a weaker sense of self.

Age 18 to 25

YOUNG ADULTS START to fall in love. Successfully developing a close relationship with other people forms intimacy. They gain the ability to *love*.

Failure to maintain a lasting relationship causes loneliness and isolation.

Age 25 to 50

MIDDLE-AGED ADULTS WANT to do things that outlast them, such as having children or contributing to the world. They acquire *kindness* to share their concerns with the next generation.

Those who fail to gain generativity stagnate. They feel shallowness in their life.

Age 50 to Death

OLDER ADULTS REMINISCE about their achievements to feel a sense of fulfillment. The *integrity* they have must reconcile with what they have done. They develop their own *perspective* from wisdom accumulated over their lifespan.

Failing to gain a sense of a life well-lived brings individuals in this last age group despair and feelings of regret over not accomplishing what they should have.

WHILE MATURITY generally leads to more improved character traits, this reference shall not be treated as a perfect step to developing character strengths. I think humans have the capacity to develop character strengths at different phases of life, depending upon their innate attitude and upbringing. Children in a war zone may form the empathy to *love* earlier. Likewise, a quinquagenarian may not reflect on past contributions to form an objective *perspective*.

External Influence

A person's character is influenced heavily by his environment. The old saying that you are the sum of your five closest friends is not far from the truth. Psychologists call it the *proximity effect*.

Stemming from our biological need to belong, we always want to fit in to ensure our survival. Social conformity has been shown to be a survival instinct. It takes willpower to fight the influence our environment exudes. For example, if your office culture plays the blame game, you begin to internalize it. It takes even more willpower to fight the influence that favors instant gratification. If all your housemates and school friends play video games, the pull to play one grows stronger each day.

KIPP (the Knowledge Is Power Program) is a network of charter schools educating low-income and minority students from early childhood to high school in the United States. The program is designed with only one goal in mind, and that is preparing students for college. Each classroom is named after a college school. Teachers deliver carefully crafted pep talks to send subliminal messages to the students. One of the daily routines includes chanting motivational and educational slogans. Every day, students receive a signal that says, "There is no time to waste; better get busy."

The school issues a halt-stop order whenever students commit a mistake or misbehave. Generally, this order is given to students who are failing to meet academic expectations or who are engaging in unacceptable behavior such as failing to fill in their name on a homework submission or bullying friends. Well-behaved or academically bright students are rewarded with a fun field trip.

Students must maintain a high level of discipline. They've got to do whatever it takes to cope with the school's workload. The school has long study hours, from 7:30 a.m. to 5 p.m. from Monday to Saturday. Its students spend 67% more time in class than regular public-school students. Teachers are available by phone to help with any afterschool questions until 9 p.m. Students are held to a high academic standard. No excuses.

Besides producing highly disciplined and academically successful students since its inception, KIPP has sent 38% of its low-income students to college, compared to just about 9 percent from public schools. The rigorous curriculum and unique approach to education at KIPP schools have led to consistently high test scores for the network, as well as increased graduation rates for its students.

Whether you are aware of it, where you live matters a lot to your personality. The more you surround yourself with positive people, the more you resemble them.

Turn your home into a talent hotbed for your children by creating an environment that favors positive characters. Don't smoke if you don't want your children to smoke. Do the things you know you should do, even when you do not want to do them, if you want your children to cultivate high self-discipline. Hold a high moral standard if you want your children to foster honesty and integrity.

TRAIN yourself to develop the required strengths that can bring out the best in you. This will not only make you better equipped to deal with challenges in your own life but will also make you a more well-rounded person to carry out your life's task. People with a diverse range of strengths are often more successful in both their personal and professional lives.[5]

3

SKILL

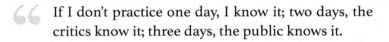 If I don't practice one day, I know it; two days, the critics know it; three days, the public knows it.

— JASCHA HEIFETZ

SKILL IS THE QUALITY OF BEING ABLE TO DO SOMETHING WELL AND proficiently. Skill is not endowed to us at birth. It is something we must learn and work at perfecting.

Throughout life, we can develop and learn skills that will help us survive and thrive in our environment. The skills we need to navigate our lives are vastly different from the ones needed centuries ago.

- The Neanderthals learned to control fire, giving them a major advantage over other animals and allowing them to cook food, stay warm, and create light.
- The Mayans learned a complex system of writing, mathematics, and astronomy to build stunning art and architecture.
- The Inuit people of the Arctic learned to fish on the ice to sustain themselves.

The ability to develop new skills allows us to adapt to our ever-changing environment. This ability allows us to change our behavior or thinking patterns to better cope with new situations.

Drawing is now digitized so Pablo Picasso's skill alone may not have been revered had his work emerged in the twenty-first century because many people can now use computers to create art that looks just as good as his paintings. If Picasso were alive today, he would have to adapt his style and abilities with the proliferation of digital art. The Spanish-born artist might not make it through the art world today if he denounced computers as he did in 1968. As technology advances, so does the art that is created.

The pursuit of one's life's work requires knowledge of the relevant skills involved. You cannot forgo learning these skills.

The 10,000-Hour Rule

Skill is acquired through learning and practicing. There's no doubt that becoming a master of any skill takes a lot of time and effort. Even if you're naturally talented or have a knack for a certain activity, it still takes years of deliberate practice to become a true expert.

The Swedish researcher K. Anders Ericsson found that many world-class athletes practice between three and a half and four hours a day. Malcolm Gladwell advocated the "10,000-hour rule" as the key to achieving true expertise.[1] That would be around nine years if you spend three hours practicing every day. It is worth knowing that the 10,000-hour is not a hard rule.[2] It is an average of what most top performers need to excel. Everyone progresses at a different rate. The quality of practice matters more than the quantity thereof.[3]

László Polgár, a researcher, conducted an experiment with his three daughters to make them world-class chess players. Even though Laszlo was not a skilled chess player, he home-schooled and taught his daughters chess. His elder daughter, Susan Polgár, beat all her opponents 10-0 in a tournament where the participants were adults. By fifteen, she was the top-ranked female chess player in the world. The International Chess Federation awarded her the title of Grandmaster when she was twenty-two.[4] Laszlo's two younger daughters went on to become renowned chess players. Judit became the Grandmaster and Sophia the International Master.

This experiment shows how the 10,000-hour rule can be used to groom world-class performers. But there is a flaw. It appears to be only applicable in competitions that have well-established rules but little room for creativity. In chess, tennis, or baseball, there are only so many possible moves that players can use. With enough practice, you develop an instinctual ability to predict an opponent's next moves. The games are so rigid that luck plays very little into winning.

The 10,000-hour rule enables us to master a well-established task that allows us to compete on the world stage. With continuous practice, a badminton player can eventually become the best in the world. However, it does not apply to activities with a high level of creativity such as writing, painting, composing music, or doing business. These creative tasks do not have a static end goal that you can practice toward. You cannot get better linearly through a continuous grind. Putting the popularity factor aside, a musician does not necessarily produce another masterpiece after producing one, no matter how much training he continues to get. Picasso did not produce another groundbreaking painting after *Guernica*.

Creative work requires you to produce something original and novel, which means the goal is reflective of us and our times, which are ever-changing.[5] There are many skilled artists who can paint the *Mona Lisa* now, but those works are valueless because they are not original. When Leonardo da Vinci painted the *Mona Lisa* during the Renaissance period, his work was an innovation. Anyone can learn the technical aspects of painting with long hours of practice, but that won't give them the creative capability.

One night, Stephenie Meyer dreamed about a girl falling in love with a vampire. The story was so intricate that she woke up and started writing the five-hundred-page book *Twilight*. That series of books had sold over 100 million copies.

Meyer had little experience in writing. *The New York Times* criticized the novel, claiming it suffered from amateurish writing. The author did not know much about vampires when she wrote her novel. In mythology, vampires are well known for sleeping during the daytime, but Meyer's vampire, Edward, does not sleep at all. She decided not to fix this *error* in her subsequent books as the story had already taken shape. After all, if Edward slept in the daytime, there would have been no school setting in the book during which he could meet and fall in love with Bella.

The book won the market because its story resonated with teen fantasies about falling in love. And it was all done without the author having to commit 10,000 hours of practice. If she had followed the well-established rules and made her vampire the same as all the rest, *Twilight* may not be as famous as it is now.

Doing business has no rules and requires a lot of creativity. The game is capricious and moves with economic climates, government policies, technological advancements, and trends. Luck plays an important role in succeeding. A relatively inexperienced newcomer, Apple, was able to dethrone Nokia, a decade-long behemoth in the mobile industry.

In the realm of creative work, spending too much time learning can actually diminish the result.[6] After a tipping point, the more you learn, the less creative you become.[7] Your work becomes more rigid because you naturally try to adopt what you learn. Your brain becomes less receptive to possibilities that do not seem *correct*; it impedes your intuition. You become so entrenched in your habitual way of thinking that you miss seeing opportunities from other perspectives. That's why some very intelligent people fail, and some mediocre people rise.

Countless experts have failed to innovate.[8] IBM, which is known for its computer hardware and software, failed to foresee the potential of the personal computer, which would someday sit on every worker's desk instead of just in the server room. Nokia was the undisputed king of mobile phones and refused to adopt touchscreens in favor of traditional buttons. This decision cost them dearly in the marketplace. William Orton of Western Union failed to recognize the value of telephones.

It stands to reason that not only does the 10,000-hour rule not work in creative tasks but physical limitations also constrain it. A shorter person, like me, who trains for over 10,000 hours will still lose to a Kenyan with the physical advantage of lighter, longer, and more slender legs, slender arms, and a shorter torso who trains for just under 1,000 hours for a long-distance race. I don't possess the innate abilities and attributes that would put me in an advantageous position to compete in such a race, and therefore, spending 10,000 hours to improve my weaknesses would be a waste of time.

Brick by Brick

As humans, the two natural processes that we must constantly engage in are growing and learning. The ability to learn any skill increases with the study and application of that skill. Because of the plasticity of your brain, the more you learn, the more your brain gets better at it, which lets you learn even more. The brain doesn't just store information passively—it actively uses what it has learned to optimize future learning.

The benefits of learning don't just stop there. By expanding your knowledge base, you open yourself up to new opportunities and experiences that would otherwise be inaccessible to you. Increased knowledge also gives you the insight to use your skills in a creative and satisfying way to solve problems or tackle new challenges.

You are bound to make mistakes on your journey, which will be filled with trials and errors, but knowledge can prevent you from making expensive mistakes and propel you to your destination fast. You will be able to make faster decisions and correct your course more quickly than those with less knowledge because of a greater understanding of the subject.

Assimilate wisdom from the world's best minds. Nowadays, books are cheap and knowledge is almost freely available and shared in abundance. You don't always have access to world-class mentors, but thankfully, many have published books. You can consume their experience and knowledge through their books even though the experience is not as personalized as it would be with access to a mentor directly.

Rapid Skills Acquisition

Acquiring new skills takes a lot of time and effort. However, with the right approach, it is possible to learn new skills quickly. There are a few key things that you can do to learn new skills more rapidly by utilizing the power of brain plasticity.

1. Slow and deep practice

SPEED PRACTICING CAN BOOST your confidence and make it feel like you are mastering a subject quickly, but it actually reduces deliberation significantly. Deep practice requires you to practice slowly, learn the granular level of each part, and correct any mistake as you go. Only when you practice slowly can you attend more closely to errors.

There is a part of your brain that plays a critical role in skills acquisition called myelin. Myelin is a substance that coats your nerve cells and helps them send signals through your brain. The more myelin you have, the faster and more efficiently your brain cells' signals travel as they communicate with each other. When you repeatedly get the sequence of practice right, your myelin becomes more efficient at getting all the steps right the next time. The more times you make that perfect golf swing, the easier it gets for you to do it again. That is how myelin expedites skills acquisition.

Note: Breastfed babies have higher myelin levels than non-breastfed ones since breastmilk fatty acids build myelin.[9]

If you are learning to play the violin or piano, you must develop the uncanny ability to detect any slight mistake in your practice and correct it at the right time. A good coach is instrumental in this process because he can spot your mistake while you are performing. Learn your craft with the same precision and care as a medical student examines each molecule of a cadaver.

When you master the smallest part of learning, your brain becomes more efficient in memorizing the pattern. Your brain recognizes each smaller group in the subject as one unit, as your understanding of the subject deepens. As you continue practicing deep learning, you gradually group smaller units as well. Each successful practice of a smaller group's units precedes the mastery of the bigger group's units. This makes you extremely fast in acquiring the skill. A skilled chess player sees the pattern of movement faster than a novice player because of this.[10]

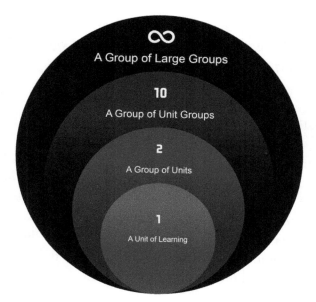

Our Brain on Learning Units

However, such a glacial pace of persnickety practice can feel very demotivating, at least at the beginning. While all your friends are already learning some fancy piece of music, you are still trundling along at the same beginner's pace. But, as you fully master each element of the music, you can produce a lasting result. Your subsequent progress can feel like a quantum leap.

That being stated, educational videos widely marketed as helpful tools to improve childhood education may actually hamper learning, especially for children aged three and younger.[11] The images and sounds are entertaining, but there is no opportunity for deep practice in which children can identify and correct mistakes. Children learn more when they are given the opportunity to interact with the real world. A 2007 study conducted by the University of Washington revealed that watching brain science children's videos for one hour daily diminished the vocabulary of children ages eight to sixteen months by 17%.[12]

2. Repetition

EVERY TIME you practice a certain skill, your brain cells form a connection with one another and make the connection stronger. The stronger the connection, the easier it is to fire the circuit and make the same movement/learning/practice next time. Human babies get good at walking not by their age or brain development but by the number of times they repeatedly spend firing the same circuit to walk.[13]

Our brain continuously purges unused connections formed throughout our lives. As you stop firing the same neurons (or brain cells) used to practice, the neuron connections weaken. This makes sense evolutionarily. Your brain's primary goal is to keep you alive. When you stop learning a skill, it is thought of as no longer necessary for your survival. Your brain needs to channel its energy to master other skills or habits that you do repeatedly.

Ergo, one way to deteriorate a world-class performer is to deprive him of practice, which will stop his brain from firing the circuit.

When IQ Scores Are an Obstacle

Being told that you have a low IQ score may leave you feeling discouraged. You may be reluctant to pursue any dream because you don't feel you have the capacity to achieve it. A low IQ score may seem like a death sentence to your chances of success.

This continuous, self-defeating thinking generates a vicious cycle that indwells in your subconsciousness. What you believe to be the truth becomes the prophecy. Read the fourth book in the series *Peak Mindset* to learn more about the workings of our subconscious.

It's a saddening reality that many people are still trapped in this belief. An IQ score is never a predictor of success, no matter how it is romanticized in the education world. While a person's IQ may indicate an important academic aptitude, it is not the be-all and end-all. A high IQ makes answering problems with only one correct answer easier, such as solving algebra, but our increasingly complex world needs creative solutions that have no one right answer.[14]

There are multiple qualities we possess that, when nurtured properly, can easily compensate for lack of IQ as we take on the world. Some highly successful people with low IQs have used their gift in a unique way to achieve great things such as Muhammad Ali, the world champion boxer; Richard Feynman, the physicist and Nobel Prize laureate; and Abraham Lincoln, the president who changed America's history forever. We can capitalize on our skills and unique character traits to flourish.

Remember that you have a gift that makes you unique. Don't compare yourself to others or try to fit into a mold that doesn't fit you.

Creativity

Creativity is an important part of any field. In today's era, a problem with an obvious solution would have likely been solved by others. Problems that are solvable with technical skills alone are already peppered with many accessible solutions. If you want to solve the world's problems, coalesce your unique gift by developing creative solutions to problems. With your gift, use the latest technologies/discoveries/sciences at your disposal innovatively to solve an unmet need that may not be apparent (yet).

Instead of buying rocket parts from subcontractors who charge insane prices for space-certified parts, SpaceX mass produces its own rocket parts. This allows SpaceX to produce rockets that are far cheaper than contemporary alternatives. These cost-effective rockets have enabled NASA to increase space exploration and discovery.

Creative skills, combined with experience and a deep technical knowledge of multiple fields, empower you to synthesize unthinkable solutions. Atsushi Tero used slime molds to find the most efficient route for network traffic. He used a creative application of his biology knowledge to solve a transportation problem.

OUR BRAIN HAS TWO HEMISPHERES: left and right. The left hemisphere controls the right part of our body, while the right hemisphere controls the left. The limbic system and the prefrontal cortex are separated into halves within the left and right hemispheres. Our prefrontal cortex is the region of the brain that handles executive functions, allowing us to make decisions, analyze complex behaviors, and solve problems. This is the conscious brain. Our limbic system is the region of our brain that is responsible for emotions, motivation, aggression, and survival. Our impromptu actions are derived from this part of the brain. This is where our subconscious operates.

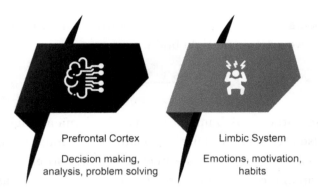

Prefrontal Cortex

Decision making, analysis, problem solving

Limbic System

Emotions, motivation, habits

Cognitive System

Many of us have been led to think, due to popular belief, that a creative person's right hemisphere is the more dominant part of their brain. Left-handed people are thought to be more creative, while right-handed ones are more analytical. This is based on research that suggests that the right hemisphere of the brain is more active in performing creative tasks. While there is no definitive proof of this theory, it is intriguing enough to warrant further exploration.

Despite language being more left-oriented and emotional responses being more right-oriented, there is no evidence to suggest that one side of a person's brain is more dominant than the other. Neither the left nor right hemisphere is used exclusively for any activity.[15] Several brain regions are put to use when you pay attention to music, immersing yourself in the rhythm and following the melody.

An amateur musician uses mostly his right hemisphere when he first starts practicing.[16] This is because, at this point, he isn't being pressured to play the music perfectly. He can afford to be playful and explore. As the musician turns pro, he plays with an acute awareness of the audience and his own performance, making sure to give the best show possible. This utilizes the left hemisphere more. Therefore, it is not true that creative people must have a dominant right brain.

IT IS important to debunk the myth of the dominant right brain because it can lead to false expectations for children who are deemed to be creative. One may be tempted to enhance the right brain for its almighty creative skills and forfeit analytical skills. Right-brain training promises to enable children to acquire a photographic memory, speed reading abilities, and other talents. These claims may seem like they would be beneficial for those labeled as creative, but in reality, they may just lead to frustration if the promised abilities do not happen naturally.

The frequent exposure to the rapid movement of flashcards—an effect similar to watching TV—does more harm than good to children's brain development.[17] Their ability to work on tasks that require high concentration reduces.

Such training promises the capacity to gain a photographic memory, even though there is no evidence of its efficacy. The children may get better at memorizing the flashcards, but memorization is not to be confused with learning. Furthermore, the capacity to memorize flashcards is not transferable to other areas of learning. The children become good just at memorizing flashcards, not necessarily other elements.[18]

It is important not to over-emphasize one side of our brain at the expense of the other, and therefore, the abilities it represents. Creativity is a multifaceted skill that does not involve only one brain region while discrediting the other. Both left and right brains are always in play.[19] To pull our creative juice together and make it really work, we need to oscillate between the left brain's analytical prowess and the right brain's creative imagination.[20]

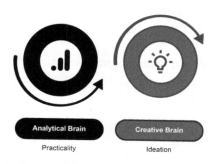

Analytical and Creative Brain Working Together

Creative solutions are derived from the intuition that our subconscious mind sparks.[21] However, analytical thinking plays an important role in getting those solutions to fruition. When an idea emerges, you need to use your analytical skills to assess its applicability to the real world. Your analytical brain needs to filter out the most obvious ideas and recall any previously tried solutions for you to generate the most original idea. Your ideas need to make sense to the world. If your creative skills open up broadly enough to allow in idea generation, your analytical skills can narrow these ideas down to ones that are usable.

Most mentally ill people are also highly creative; the only problem is that their ideas may not be highly practical in the real world.[22] A dementia patient who loses much of his left brain's analytical capacity can generate a lot of creative ideas. However, without the capability to evaluate the ideas, the ideas are useless.

Creative people can, with great flexibility, use the left and right brain, which means they can harness analytical and creative thinking—their conscious and subconscious cognitive system —depending on which one is the most useful at the moment.

Creativity is enhanced:

- When we let our mind roam free with no logical thought
- When our mind wanders as opposed to being mindful
- When we are playful instead of being serious
- When we take a bold risk instead of deliberating
- When we deal with novelty instead of quality
- When our thought is more chaotic instead of controlled
- When we try unfamiliar experiences instead of following routines

Optimal creative skill development can be acquired through repeated engagement in creative work: writing, reading, playing, singing, creating, or taking healthy risks. Regrettably, young children are fed a passive consumption of social media and learning applications that favor extrinsic rewards. Children grow up learning only to take up the work that produces the most money, not necessarily the kind of work they like doing. This proves to be detrimental to solving creative problems.

Lifetime Skill Development

Skills developed since childhood bloom into potential career opportunities as we enter adulthood. Young John Davison Rockefeller raised turkeys to earn money. He saved money to buy a bag of candy and then sold it in individual pieces to earn a profit. At seven, he saved up $50 to loan to farmers at a 7% interest rate. His father encouraged him to pursue business, and so he attended a business course after completing two years of high school.

Rockefeller later partnered with a fellow businessman to form a company that dealt with grain, hay, meat, and other items. The business was profitable in the first year even with heavy competition. Rockefeller went on to become a billionaire oil baron and one of the most successful industrialists in the history of the United States.

Rockefeller's industrious spirit had been apparent in childhood, and instead of repressing it, he honed it with the support of his parents. Countless success stories involving people whose skills were nurtured in childhood can be found in any field. Parents of many Nobel Prize winners enriched their children with books, experimental work, and scientific toys. Olympian athletes' parents tend to support their children's sport. There are numerous accounts of parents ferrying these budding athletes to practice, sacrificing downtime, and offering help and influence as their kids toiled away in search of glory.

By fostering your skills early in life, you can take advantage of opportunities that come your way and create a positive trajectory toward success. There is no better time to start developing your skills than now.

SKILL DEVELOPMENT REQUIRES TIME, effort, and deep practice. Any skill can be learned whether or not you have the talent for it. Don't be discouraged from pursuing complex skills because you think you don't have the talent. Take on challenging projects that stretch you beyond your current capabilities. This will help build your skills while providing new challenges that keep you engaged. Besides, you will learn more from taking on a complex project that you are not quite ready for than from doing the same thing over and over that you no longer enjoy.

4

INTEREST

The intellect is a great danger to creativity because you begin to rationalize and make up reasons for things instead of staying with your own basic truth–who you are, what you are, what you wanna be.

— RAY BRADBURY

IN TIMES PAST, MORE PEOPLE, IN GENERAL, STRUGGLED MORE TO determine exactly what they wanted out of life, likely due to less exposure to information and to the world overall. In our current age, however, a good grasp of life goals is far more common. With so much information at our fingertips, it can be hard to know where to start when figuring out our interest. Once we do determine this, however, it can be used to build relationships, find work that fits us, and more.

Indications of Our Interest

All of us have interests in at least a few things. In fact, if we don't have any interest at all, it may indicate a personality disorder.

You know you have a profound interest in something if:

1. You are so absorbed in a singular thing that you lose awareness of time passing
2. You are so eager to do a particular thing that you don't mind sacrificing your time and money
3. Your curiosity heightens when you do that certain thing
4. You listen to, read about, or intensely watch information about that subject
5. You want to learn about it despite it being a tough topic
6. You spend hours researching that topic
7. When you fail at something, you happily retry
8. You are naturally drawn to the subject

Pay attention to these signs as you navigate through your life. No matter how unusual your particular interest may be, it will serve as the seed to your life's work.

Look through your childhood; find what piqued your interest, even if it may have been suppressed growing up. Consider the things that you always go back to, no matter the circumstances. Something that brightens your day. Note the following inclinations that enliven you but may be mistaken as your natural interest:

1. Instant gratification

IT IS easy to confuse an innate ability with a dopamine-driven interest such as playing video games or watching TV. You could have a high interest in them because you are using them to satisfy your desire for gratification; therefore, you get good at doing them.

Interest is a good guiding star toward discovering your strengths but should be carefully discerned from that which satisfies your want. Instant gratification is usually an escape from boredom. We are bored when we stagnate. When we are not working on our true abilities. After consuming the pleasure, however, we remain shallow.

2. Your job

THE TASKS that you do with ease at work are not necessarily your talents. It may be just the subset. You may be quick to confirm that your strength is anchoring news because you are already doing it and have gained a lot of praise in the process. Presenting may also be one of your strengths, but maybe your talent is really "writing a persuasive speech."

Competency in the tasks required by your job scope does not always reflect what you really enjoy doing. This can make it even more difficult for most of us to see through to our actual interest.

Transforming Interest into One's Life's Work

 Everything I do is completely original—I made it up when I was a little kid.

— CLAES OLDENBURG

Your childhood interest and experience play critical roles in stockpiling materials for your creative work. Early in life, your brain craves intellectual stimulation that matches your cognitive abilities. Unleashing its craving and cultivating your interest at a young age stimulates creative imagination that will become useful later in life.

As a child, Shigeru Miyamoto was an interest in exploring natural areas around his home. One day he found a cave, went inside, and found that it led to another cavern. Inspired by his childhood wonderment, he grew up creating the iconic Mario Bros. video game, featuring a plumber who can teleport around islands and worlds through warp pipes to rescue a princess.

The Brontë siblings wrote *Jane Eyre* and created the complex popular fantasy graphic novel *Glass Town* while still teenagers. That novel was read by millions. The Brontë sisters lived in England and had a creative childhood with access to a lot of books. Their father was an Anglican clergyman, and their mother was a poet. The sisters were educated at home by their parents. They spent their summers at their family home, near Haworth, Yorkshire, where they relished reading, writing, painting, playing music, and hiking. Their mother was driven to support her children's literary ambitions. From an early age, the siblings were encouraged to write.

When Richard Branson was twelve, he planted Christmas trees in his backyard to sell at a profit. The saplings were eaten by rabbits, which ruined his business plan. That first entrepreneurial failure seeded his entrepreneurship journey and fueled his drive to become successful.

When you engage in your interest through play, your brain becomes primed for creative problem-solving. You are experimenting with your curiosity and focusing it on something unfamiliar to make it familiar.[1] Bring your childhood imaginary world alive by transcribing it into a novel. Sculpt your magical life into a work of art. Act out your favorite fantasy stories in a play.

Unfortunately, most parents tend to push their children into academic learning. In 1955, playtime began to be considered an unnecessary part of learning and was reduced.[2] This not only takes the fun out of learning but also suppresses children's creative imaginations, making them less curious and less likely to coalesce new ideas.[3]

We may have put the wrong emphasis on children's development by prioritizing academic skills before free play. Research shows that children who learn to read later have better reading comprehension compared to those who learn to read earlier.[4] As children grow up spending more time in serious studies, they tend to lose interest in fun. They lose their natural instinct to imagine and create. Building up children's natural curiosity and creativity establishes the foundation to support their academic learning.

You, too, have grown up with multiple interests. Some may have been discarded as you aged because they were aberrant; for example, interest in spiders, pigeon racing, or trainspotting. With varying skills and interests, you can gain meaning from your inner and outer experiences and bring them both together in a novel way or find an unusual way to produce a fresh idea.

Inject some playful time into your daily grind to keep your creativity flowing and your motivation tank full for serious work.[5] You will hit upon inspiration more often when feeling creative than when you are being serious. Aha moments occur when you least expect them. Remember, there is no interest too odd to ignore—just as Shigeru showed us by his interest in caves. When you have interests you're passionate about, you have something to look forward to, which enables you to build a life's work that can contribute to the world.

Interest Killers

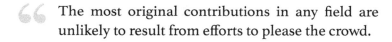 The most original contributions in any field are unlikely to result from efforts to please the crowd.

— ROBERT STERNBERG

Your interests give you something to focus on and look forward to. If you are not careful, your interests can wane without your knowledge. Some things that can kill your interests:

1. Extrinsic rewards

THE MAGIC of doing work out of pure joy is truly rewarding. But most of us let external rewards ruin that joy. People who are paid to perform a task, either through money or prizes, are less likely to enjoy the task for its own sake and, as a result, are less likely to devote their free time to it. The task is seen as a way to get something, not as something they enjoy. When the reward is no longer present, they dread the task.

You may feel compelled to alter your unique writing voice because statistics show others are more popular. When you proceed with the change, you realize that you cease being yourself and can't do what you do best.

Rather than playing at your best when you join a sports competition, you play just in the hope of gaining the prestige associated with winning a trophy. Thus, you generate anxiety and fear that reduces your focus to compete.

External rewards kill motivation. Gifting young children money for studying well destroys the fun of learning. Gifting adult children with regular monetary subsidies demotivates them to be independent. Well-intentioned purposes, but paradoxical outcomes. Never let external sources conquer your interests.

2. Lack of a challenge

TO DEVELOP AN INTEREST IN ANYTHING, there must be a challenge to push us out of our comfort zones and inspire us to do better. The challenge should involve things we want to learn more about, explore, and experience.

If there is no opposition, the interest will eventually dissipate. If you are a tennis player, without a challenge, you will quickly lose interest in the game and may even give up altogether. To keep your interest piqued, you need opponents who match your skill level. With enough competition, you can stay motivated and engaged in your sport, all while having fun.

3) The task is too challenging

JUST AS A BANAL environment shrinks your interest, challenges that are too hard can kill it too. If you can't score any shots in a match, you eventually give up out of frustration because you feel that you have no control over the outcome.

To maintain interest, the challenge of the work must be made progressively more difficult. This is evident in both physical and intellectual challenges that are put before those who partake in a challenging activity. For example, if someone were to go skiing for the first time, they would likely go at a slower pace at first to avoid falling and injuring themselves. As they get better and more confident on the slopes, their speed gradually increases until they reach their peak level of skiing ability. In a similar way, intellectual challenges should also become progressively harder as one becomes better acquainted with them. This is especially true for subjects like mathematics or science, where people may be comfortable with basic concepts but may not be able to tackle harder problems.

4. Lack of engagement

LACK OF ENGAGEMENT in your interest can stem from a variety of factors such as boredom or lack of opportunity. It can also be due to a lack of knowledge or understanding about the topic. If you feel you don't have what it takes to learn more about an interest, you may be less likely to take part.

Children today have far fewer opportunities to engage in their interests than their predecessors did.[6] When they have no opportunity to engage in what interests them, they lose touch with those interests. This is often the case when parents discourage their children's interests to steer them toward more conventional pursuits such as education or a career. While this approach may be motivated by love, it kills their children's passions. Ideally, parents should encourage their children to explore their interests without feeling pressure to conform to traditional norms.

As you learn more about your chosen field of interest, you will naturally become more interested in it. The more knowledge you have, the more you will be able to apply it in your chosen field, and the more competent you will feel. This increased knowledge and competence will, in turn, lead to even more interest in the subject.

Having a well-developed interest deepens your affection for a particular task, which increases your motivation. Your engagement increases, helping you to withstand any frustration the work may present. This lays fertile ground for you to persevere throughout your life's work, which inevitably will be met by adversities. Cultivate your interests, whatever they may be, for they are the ingredients to innovation and an interesting life.

5

TALENT

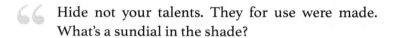 Hide not your talents. They for use were made. What's a sundial in the shade?

— BENJAMIN FRANKLIN

THERE ARE THOSE AMONG US WHO ARE GIFTED WITH EXCEPTIONAL talent. For some, it is a gift for music, art, or mathematics. Others have a natural prowess for athletics. Whatever the form, talent is something that comes with us and sets us apart from the rest. Talent is sometimes confused with skills. Talent is your unique inborn special ability, while skill is an expertise acquired through learning.

For those of us lucky enough to have found our talent, it is our responsibility to nurture it and make the most of it. We should never take our talents for granted but use them to make a difference in the world. With hard work and dedication, we can turn our talents into something truly special.

- You may have a talent for perfect pitch and a skill for playing the piano. Together, they make you a wonderful pianist.
- You may have a talent for numerical reasoning and a skill in mathematical problem-solving. Together, they make you a great statistician.
- You may have a talent for visuospatial imagination and a skill for solving geometric problems. Together, they make you an excellent architect.

No matter how uncomfortable it is to discuss, your talent plays a big part in influencing your success. Make no mistake, however, that it does not mean average people cannot beat the genius. It's just that the genius requires less practice time than the non-genius does to gain the same level of skills.

The Freedom of Expression

During your childhood, you were free to explore the world. You could roam a garden to find different types of beetles that fascinated you. You could be intrigued by the magic of the moving object that you stared at the waterfall intently. You might spend hours tinkering with a mechanical device until it reaches the perfect level of functionality. When you were a child, you weren't worried about wasting time. You had all the time in the world to do what you liked.

Your talent became the most profound during childhood, when your desire was still unadulterated by worldly influence or the stigma that surrounds certain talents. You continued to do what you did because you wanted to—even if it did not earn you a penny. Your natural talent emanated so that it became conspicuous to many.

These inclinations diminished and became more difficult for others to notice as you grew older. You created more rigid rules for yourself, unlike when you were still trying to discover who you were during your childhood. You wanted to develop an identity—one that was preferably acceptable by the surrounding people in your world. Your proclivity was influenced by your environment, your parents' expectations, and social norms.

You repressed your natural talent if it seemed odd and did not belong to your newfound world of adulthood. The people around you seemed more and more conservative the older you got. They looked up to people with power and authority. Their primary goal was to be accepted and recognized in their own community. You were told to abandon your childish behavior and play the role of a responsible adult. You knew you had a talent that was a part of you, but you did not want to be associated with that "child."

Latent Talent

We have a natural tendency to romanticize high-achievers as talented individuals. It may be hard to believe that you have a talent when you have done nothing groundbreaking while many others accomplish things far greater than what you've ever done. You may have suffered so many defeats that you can't believe you have any talent at all.

Being a non-genius in a field is not disadvantageous because it means you are a genius at something else. It means there is an unexplored opportunity in you that you haven't discovered yet. You have something else that is not commonly seen in the world. And that usually results in a breakthrough once the world realizes—and is surprised by—your talent.

Helen Keller was born in 1880 as a normal, healthy child. Then she suffered an unknown illness at nineteen months old, leaving her deaf and blind and shaping the rest of her life. As a young child, she had a strong desire to speak out but couldn't join in any conversations with others. She went on to create a kind of sign language to help her communicate.

At seven, Helen met Anne Sullivan, who taught her finger spelling to communicate with ease. Anne became Helen's mentor and teacher. As years went by, she learned how to do things other people couldn't without relying on somebody else for help, like learning braille at eight years old.

Helen later was accepted into Radcliffe College in Cambridge, and with Anne's help, learned how to interpret the study material. In 1904, at just the age of twenty-four, Helen Keller earned her bachelor's degree. This made her the first deaf-blind person to accomplish this feat and enabled her to travel, giving speeches about everything from going blind to understanding speech by reading people's lips. She became an author and advocate for people with disabilities.

There would have been no way anyone would have thought someone with severe disabilities could accomplish so much. It was inconceivable. Through her disadvantages, Helen discovered her talent, created a fulfilling life for herself, and transcended her life's work to better the world.

MOST OF US are unaware of our talent's existence because it is not always clear. As a natural part of our life, it does not seem like a gift until we witness others who do not have our acute hearing abilities or who take longer to solve spatial problems.

We are not all born with the same potential, but we can always take steps toward developing our dormant talents.

There are gifts that aren't immediately apparent. Some gifts are obfuscated from your awareness because you lack the opportunity to showcase them. You may have a gift that's wasted in your current environment because it's not valued. For example, you might be a marketing genius in an organization that doesn't care about marketing.

Sometimes we are too blind to realize what our special abilities are, and this can lead us to miss out on our true talents. It is, thus, important that you remain open to doing things you don't normally do to increase the likelihood of stumbling upon your gift.

Discover Your Talents

In finding and developing your talent, there are certain signs to look out for. It is important to be aware of these signs so that you can better develop your talent and reach your full potential. Look for such signs as:

1. You are excited to show the talent to others, especially at first.
2. All your projects revolve around using that talent.
3. You feel like you are being your true self when you exercise that talent.
4. You can't avoid using that talent in most of the things you do. It is intrinsic in you to use it whether there is a reward for using it.
5. It is invigorating (not draining) whenever you use your talent to work on something. Using your talents gives you energy and makes you feel fulfilled. Pay attention to the activities that make you feel most alive and engaged.
6. With practice, you can progress more rapidly than other individuals can.
7. You know that if you put your mind to it, you will eventually find a way to solve the problem.

Listen to your intuition and notice the things that you are naturally good at. Maintain the list as you go on. Keep note of these signs. Reminisce about your past accomplishments, the things you have succeeded at easily. Whenever you are aware of a specific thing you are capable of effortlessly, but others find difficult, that's an indication of your talent.

The signals come in different ways. They can be so subtle that you may find them hard to notice because you've become blasé about living with them. Perhaps you are drawn toward shapes or drawing or song lyrics. No matter what you do, your natural inclination is always there, waiting for you to nurture it to full potential.

Ask trusted friends, family, or colleagues for their honest feedback about your strengths and weaknesses. This can give you valuable insights into your talents.

As you look back at the experiences in your life that energized you, you will end up with an extensive list of possibilities. Find the commonalities among them. Scrutinize them until you find something that makes sense in the grand scheme of things. For example, perhaps you enjoyed developing software that could run at the fastest possible speed. You felt very satisfied when you could save ten minutes of your phone's battery consumption by tinkering with its components. You took pleasure in designing the most space-efficient kitchen layout. Rather than having a talent in software development, mobile technology, or interior design, your actual talent may be to take something that works and maximize its capabilities. You may be a maximizer.

You may find a veritable smorgasbord of talents that don't gel together during your first try. Or perhaps you have already found it but have some doubts. It is challenging to take notice of your own attributes. Alas, we judge others better than we do ourselves.[1] Try again when your thoughts are clearer.

It is essential that you don't stop there and make it your goal to find your true talents. As you do enough introspection, sooner or later, you will discover your true inner talent. When that happens, things start to make sense. You begin to realize why you do what you do and why you do it a lot. The thing that you thought was your talent may not necessarily be it. You now know that you set up a waste management business not because you have an inborn talent for dealing with waste but because you chanced upon this money-making opportunity. You've learned several foreign languages, not because of your natural talent for picking up other dialects but because you simply wanted to impress your sweetheart.

Mistaken Talents

It is common for people to confuse a great skill for a talent. Brazil has an uncannily high population of great soccer players. The number of Brazilians who play professionally around the world exceeds ten thousand.[2] Brazilians won thirty-five of thirty-eight international competitions. One may infer that these players have inborn soccer talent. Talent is a natural gift endowed at birth. To state that soccer talents are endowed in most Brazilian babies would be a statistical impossibility.

Let's look back at the lifestyle and culture of these Brazilian football legends to understand how Brazil produces the greatest footballers of all time. Brazil is an impoverished country. Many children living in favelas yearn to compete on the world stage to get out of poverty.[3] At a young age, Brazilians become obsessed with soccer. They play futsal, a game that uses a ball smaller than standard-issuer soccer balls but heavier. They play on the street, in telephone booths, in the sand, and at their home. Not on an expanse of green field, mind you.

Futsal balls, being small and bouncing less, are harder to control than soccer balls. Because it is less bouncy, the players make contact with the futsal ball more often than with a soccer ball. We have learned earlier that the combination of this deep, targeted practice (*slow practice*) combined with the twenty-hour-per-week practice sessions (*repetition*) makes skill acquisition faster than in any other method of practicing.

As a result, young Brazilians develop the dexterity and reflexes needed for ball control faster than most people. They may be revered as talented footballers around the world, but this skill acquisition is hard work—they incorporate the 10,000-hour practice technique, combined with a deep interest that produces these best players. Playing soccer is not necessarily their talent.

A Double-Edged Sword

It is worth remembering that your talent is a means to accelerate your skill acquisition. You can only gain mastery through hard work. If you are not careful, knowing what your talent is can present a disadvantage to your growth.

Complacency

We humans grow complacent easily when we have a quick fix at our fingertips, relying so much on our talent that we feel invincible. We forget the sweat that brought us to where we are now. Less talented people who dedicate their lives to mastering a skill can easily outdo the talented ones. If you have gained success easier, you tend to take things for granted.

Entitlement

If you believe that having a talent makes you deserve more success than others, you may be a victim of a fixed mindset. Fixed mindset is a psychological term that describes individuals who believe that their talents, abilities, and success are predetermined and unchangeable. Individuals with a fixed mindset often expect to be successful in the same ways, regardless of how hard they work. This can lead to feelings of entitlement and believing that one's success is due to luck or being born with certain characteristics.

Recognize your talents for what they are—finite but valuable. They can't bring you anywhere unless you cultivate them and put them to good use. Never praise your children's talent; praise their effort.

A LACK OF DESIRE TO STRUGGLE

WITH ALL THE praise showered on you for your talent, a part of you may become subconsciously afraid to lose your talent badge. Losing your newfound identity as a talented person is a threat to what you have built for yourself. You don't want to be seen struggling with a tough challenge or failing a task, both of which are ingredients for growth. You prefer to stay in your comfort zone to solve easier problems and avoid setbacks.

WITH THAT IN MIND, not knowing your talent should not stop you from pursuing your life's work. There are skills you can master. You have character strengths that you can develop. You have interests that can guide your path in life. Just like the Brazilian soccer players who might achieve extraordinary success at the sport without knowing what their talents are. All they know is to practice.

Without learning to use and enhance the talent, it will remain dormant. Your talent is a valuable resource that you can exploit to build a more productive career.

It is important to know that while knowing your true talent can give you a lot of advantages in choosing which path to undertake, not discovering one does not necessarily lead to an empty life. Developing your skills, interest, and character strengths can propel you toward the life's task you want to do. The talent may already be in your life and goals without your awareness.

NOW THAT WE have covered the three components that make up your gift, let's dive into how to synergize it to amplify its effects.

6

SYNERGIZE THE GIFT

 Chance favors only the prepared mind.

— LOUIS PASTEUR

CHARACTER STRENGTHS, INTERESTS, SKILLS, AND TALENTS FORM A gift that is uniquely yours. You bring these elements of your gift together by working on your life's work.

Character strengths define how you will execute your life's work and whether you can pursue it through to completion. Charles Darwin would not have had a chance to collect plants and bird specimens from many parts of the world to develop the theory of evolution if he had not had the social intelligence to socialize with the crews on the voyage.

Relevant skills allow you to carry out your life's work. You can't lead a troop if you have not developed the requisite leadership skills. You can't make a profit if you don't have the business acumen necessary to run your enterprise.

Interests fuel your motivation to persist during adversity. Michael Jordan may never have discovered his talent if he was more interested in baseball than basketball.

Talents help you to advance rapidly. A talent for making friends can expedite your success in an occupation that requires networking.

The Merger

For every generation, the world evolves, creating more people with diverse skills, talents, and interests. Each person uses his gift in a unique way. A person with an artistic talent may have an interest in acting, while another person may go on to become a singer. The combination of skills, talents, and interests creates a unique life's work.

Your interest in a particular work or topic increases *motivation*. Motivation fuels your desire to achieve the goals you have set for yourself.

Interest also increases your *perseverance* during difficulties, enabling you to sustain a long-haul project to successful completion. Furthermore, a task that is emotionally interesting and personally meaningful is less taxing to accomplish. The combination of both motivation and perseverance sparks *creativity* to produce new and innovative ideas or solutions for your life's work.[1]

Once you know what intrigues and motivates you, identifying the skills to invest more time in that passion becomes a breeze. Learning a skill that you are interested in can help you retain information more effectively. By focusing on the material you find interesting, you will be more likely to stay engaged in the learning process. This lets you develop new skills and knowledge faster than if you blindly pursued activities without knowing what would excite or challenge you. Besides, your interest triggers huge outflows of energy that enable you to practice your craft in greater depth, which enables rapid skills acquisition.

As you can see, once the components of your gift are synergized, it will amplify the execution of your life's work. By tapping into your gift, you can truly maximize your potential as a learner and doer.

You don't have to score off the chart on each gift before pursuing your life's task. You develop them as you work on your life's task. Each gift feeds off the others as you develop them, which creates a synergistic impact. For example, a high interest in a particular subject increases your chances of feeling inspired, which, in turn, increases your motivation to work harder to develop your skills and talents. An inquisitive character keeps your interest in knowledge high and opens you up to new opportunities.

Get Inspired

You can be inspired by reading a certain book, meeting a certain person, listening to a speech, or stumbling upon a fateful event. However, inspiration does not just occur for anybody. Many people may read that same book, meet that same person, listen to that same speech, or stumble upon that same event but remain uninspired.

A strong interest, coupled with expertise in a field, makes inspiration more accessible. The likelihood of inspiration increases because of one's openness to new ideas and opportunities.

The good news is that a strong interest in a particular field usually leads to expertise in that field. When you are interested in a field, you naturally want to work more. Work with the intent to work out of joy and solve the world's problems, not to be preoccupied with petty concerns for one's own sake. The passion and strong drive to master the work produces deep learning, and expertise mastery ensues. This loop manifests itself as increased productivity and expansion of our minds to their utmost potential.

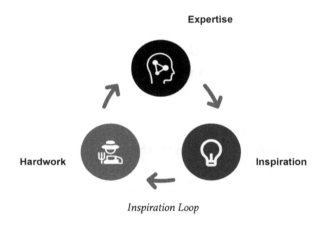

Inspiration Loop

IT DOES NOT ALWAYS HAVE to start with an interest. It is possible to develop an interest through hard work, which then triggers this inspiration loop.

Even in areas that rely on a high level of logical thinking, such as science, inspiration plays a critical role in the discovery of solutions.

Thirty-two-year-old chemist Albert Hofmann was tasked with synthesizing twenty-five chemical compounds using ergot, a fungus widely used in folklore medicine. Hofmann believed the fungus contained an active substance that could be of medical value and set his sights on discovering it.

After synthesizing the twenty-five compounds, he did not find what he was looking for. He intuited that the twenty-fifth combination, LSD-25, held something intriguing, and he relentlessly continued his research. Five years later, he attempted to re-synthesize the twenty-five compounds. At the final stage of the synthesis, a sprinkling of LSD-25 fell on Hofmann's hand, which caused a strange reaction, and he felt sick. He then proceeded to ingest a tiny dose of LSD-25. On his way home, he experienced an inexplicable feeling of oneness with nature. He found that a small dose of LSD-25 caused a psychoactive effect that alters human consciousness.

By the standards of practices conducted in the lab, any experiments that did not yield pharmacological value should have been dropped. Hofmann's interest, combined with his deep expertise, however, fueled his self-experimentation, which gave birth to a hallucinogenic drug. This is regarded as one of the greatest accidental discoveries in medical history.

Thomas Edison said that genius is one percent inspiration and ninety-nine percent perspiration. Perhaps it is time that we re-examine that equation. Inspiration and hard work feed off each other. The more you try, the more you learn. The more you learn, the more your mind opens to new possibilities that inspire you to work harder. One percent inspiration can never sustain long hours of practice and experimentation before burnout sets in.

Manufacturing Aha Moments

 All truly great thoughts are conceived by walking.

— FRIEDRICH NIETZSCHE

Sudden success for a business does not always stem from a solid business plan. A business plan is an educated guess. Planning well is impossible without knowing what you don't know yet. You never can predict the market reaction to a change of product, to emerging competitors, or to a technological advent. Most business plans do not even survive their first contact with the customer, let alone predict the company's success. Remember that doing business, producing arts, and directing movies are fluid work that requires a lot of ingenuity. The success of these endeavors hinges upon spotting the opportunity in an ocean of randomness.

Unfortunately, that skill is not something we can gain at will. When we are confronted with a problem, our brain narrows down the available solutions we have knowledge of. We're too focused on the rational aspects of solutions, as praised by the majority to be the most prudent approach to handling problems. This rigidity prevents us from looking at other unexplored solutions, ones that require creativity. If a worker is slow, we usually look at either making the worker faster or adding more workers first. Revising the process or correcting the practice to make things more efficient holistically may not be something that we look into, even if it solves the problem more effectively.

In a world where most logical solutions pale in comparison to creative ones, we need to strive to encourage more "ahas" to solve unique problems. After watching the unknown flying experiments of Otto Lilienthal, who was the first person to perform gliding flights, two brothers had a eureka moment to improve their aircraft by changing the shape of their wings. Bill Bowerman's career-defining eureka moment came one morning around breakfast in 1970 when he saw the pattern of his waffle and realized that the pattern was upside down. If the barrel had been inverted, the positive indentations on the waffle's surface could have been pressed into a surface with a sufficient grip for a non-slip sole. This gave birth to the famous Nike Waffle Racer, the running shoe without heavy spikes.

An aha moment, by its nature, is sudden, unexpected, and unpredictable. Its encounter can never be planned or deliberated. The more you strive for an aha moment, the less likely you are to encounter one. When you are using your executive functions to engage in a focused activity, your imaginative functions that are responsible for generating ideas are suppressed.[2] Fortunately, our daily routine does not require us to focus all the time. This gives us chances to stumble upon an aha moment.

The aha moment hits when your consciousness is weak, not deliberating over a problem; for example, when you are relaxing, taking a shower, or drifting off into daydreams. Your external world is temporarily shut down. Your subconscious mind roams free and taps into your memories to make possible connections from your inside world to your outside one.[3] It delves into your deepest wellsprings of creativity. The deeper the depth of knowledge you have on a particular subject, the higher the chance of your subconscious mind making a relevant connection.[4] When a connection clicks, you've hit upon an aha moment. Scientists believe this automatic process may be faster than the work of our conscious mind.[5]

The following steps lay the groundwork necessary to increase your chances of getting aha moments.

1. Use spare time to let your mind wander.

Instead of sitting in front of a computer all the time, set aside a special time and place to be outdoors. Being with nature elevates your mood and lets your mind escape the daily grind and disengage from a fixation on ineffective solutions. Many creative people can attest to its benefits. Charles Darwin brought his dog to parks. Nishida Kitaro, a philosophy professor, walked across town daily—the townspeople there even named the path Philosopher's Walk.[6] Modern research supports the finding that walking improves creativity.[7] Find secluded areas outdoors where you can escape from your daily environment. Let the aroma of grass permeate you. Let the birds' whistling guide you. Breathe in the woody scent of a wooden bench. Let the moist, warm air wash over your pores.

In his essay "Solvitur Ambulando," Charles Dickens proposed a simple solution to the problem of overthinking: Go for a walk. According to Dickens, too much time spent indoors can lead to a person becoming "stuffed full of wise sayings and maxims." Walking, on the other hand, allows for time to think without the distractions of the outside world. It is in this state of mind that we can find solutions to our problems.

When your mind wanders, it lets you communicate with your inner monologues and keeps your creative juice flowing.[8] Left to its own accord, our wandering mind naturally drifts toward the future, where we visualize our future self, scour our unfulfilled desires, and imagine our reactions to multiple scenarios.[9] This introspective process makes it likely for us to stumble upon interesting ideas. For example, in convalescence, some artists have come up with better ideas as a result of staying in bed and avoiding daily distractions.

Taking a shower temporarily creates a distance and brings your mind outside of your usual scenery and stimulations. Your mind is uninhibited by critical thought, enabling access to your subconscious memories and fantasies and shutting down the logical mind to bring out the playful mind to daydream. It is no wonder that 72% of people (including me) generate new ideas while taking a shower.[10] The Greek mathematician Archimedes discovered how to calculate the area occupied by a three-dimensional object while taking a shower. As it turns out, taking too few showers is not only harmful to hygiene but also to creativity.

Now, for your subconsciousness to harvest this connection, you need a large store of relevant memories. Relevant memories that can only be accumulated and attuned to by deep expertise of the subject. Without bolstering any deep expertise of mathematics, you can't just soak yourself in a bathtub for hours on end and expect your brain to generate insights to calculate an object's volume as Archimedes did.

2. Don't fire up your motivation when you have mixed feelings.

RESEARCH HAS FOUND that mixed intense positive and negative emotions, coupled with low motivation, make an aha moment encounter more likely. For example, the feeling of exuberance and dejection that follows winning an award but not being promoted. That ambivalent emotion primes your brain to seek novel, unusual connections, which can lead to great insight.

It shall be noted that the generation of an aha moment is only possible when you are lowly motivated. We are often taught to keep our motivation high to generate ideas. In the corporate world, business leaders often tout the benefits of setting deadlines to force creativity juice out of employees. But, as we have learned, aha moments are found when you least expect them. If your motivation to get an idea is high, your mind reduces the possibility that it will ever find any novel idea. Under the pressure of a gun, our brain's creative potential is undermined.[11] With a tight deadline approaching, employees may come up with a band-aid solution that is often confused with a creative solution.

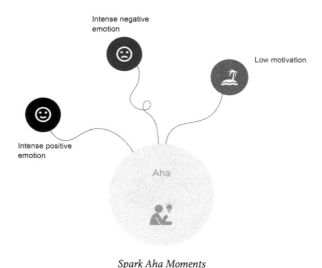

Spark Aha Moments

3. Look beyond your subject of interest.

WE ARE OFTEN TAUGHT to believe that to do our work best, we should spend as much time as possible with people in the same field. But, if you meet the same group of people from the same discipline, there is little room for serendipitous encounters. All of you share a similar history, types of work, and experiences that you are already familiar with.

Mastering just one highly specialized skill—while very useful for specialized work—inhibits innovation because you lack exposure to other potential connections. To produce an innovative solution, you need to expose yourself to a multitude of domains to bring together wisdom from various domains or interests.[12]

As counterintuitive as it sounds, you should deliberately expose yourself to something that is irrelevant to your profession.

- Mingle with new people from outside of your sphere.
- Attend a lecture on a topic outside of your expertise.
- Read books that are irrelevant to your venture.

As you do these, try to connect them with what you are already doing. Your chance of noticing an aha moment increases. When you are trying to solve a problem, your brain looks for similarities between the problem and the memories you have stored.[13] Think Nike with its Waffle Racer. The greater the range of knowledge you possess, the more you will be able to automatically come up with workable solutions that are not immediately accessible by most people.

In the late nineteenth century, the mortality rate of premature babies was about one in five. A French obstetrician, Stéphane Tarnier, suspected that proper temperature regulation would help keep premature babies alive. One day, he saw hatchlings kept inside an incubator in a zoo. He noticed the young animals needed to be kept at a certain temperature to stay alive—a process he thought could be applied to human babies too.

Tarnier convinced the zoo's poultry raiser to make him one incubator. Tarnier later introduced the incubator to the nursery of Maternité, the hospital where he worked.[14] The application of that one incubator alone increased the survival rate of premature infants by 35% to 62%. Tarnier had his aha moment after visiting a zoo and made a lasting contribution to the world of perinatal medicine.

James Harris Simons brought his impressive mathematical, scientific, and financial background together to form an illustrious hedge fund business. Leonardo da Vinci's interests in arts, science, weaponry, architecture, music, anatomy, cartography, inventing, writing, and many more subjects produced extraordinary accomplishments.

New ideas emerge when people, ideas, or experiences collide. If you stay in the same environment, same job scope, and same routine for years, your chance of discovering aha moments grows slim. To break free from the traditional way of thinking, you need to feed yourself with new experiences. It is easy to trigger a spurt of novel solutions using immigration because immigrants come from diverse backgrounds and cultures.[15]

Stroke your curious mind by spicing up your usual activities. Play new sports, go to places you've never been, attend diverse events, challenge your beliefs, or do something you've never attempted before. The novelty triggers an increased chance of sparking an epiphany and keeps you from getting fixated on your work.

Microsoft Windows 3.0 was close to being shut down because it had a terrible memory problem. David Weise, a brilliant computer scientist, was unsuccessful in finding the solution. One Friday night, Microsoft was hosting a party during the celebration of the opening of a new manufacturing plant. David Weise and Murray Sargent ran into one another and had a discussion about the memory problem. Sargent suggested that Weise bring Windows into a protected mode to free up memory and fix its memory issue. The tone of Weise's voice surprised Sargent, as he did not expect to be taken seriously. "You're absolutely correct," he implied. Weise later fixed the memory issues successfully. As a result of that Friday-night party happenstance, Windows 3.0, an almost abandoned project, became the cornerstone on which Microsoft's international empire was built.

4. Bet on the odds.

WE ARE USUALLY TOO stiff to deviate from the norm. When faced with fierce competition, we typically spearhead it with more discipline, rigor, or hard work. Trying an unusual route is usually not in our plan—after all, the ones who have succeeded before us didn't do that.

An aha moment is unpredictable. Its unpredictability cannot be exploited by following a conventional path. You will likely discover something unexpected when you place your bet on the odd strategy. Embracing disarray and taking bold risks are creative strategies.

5. Start doing.

MANY ARTISTS DISCOVER their aha moment in the process of doing the work, not before doing it. They do not think out or settle the result in advance. They don't know where they are going until they arrive there.[16]

The work continuously evolves as one's thoughts change. Many dots that were invisible at first become clearer when the artist begins painting, the perspective changes, and the viewer moves around the painting. This can often lead to fortuitous results that are even better than what the artist planned for.

Much of my best work has been the result of serendipity too. Those achievements were not planned for and certainly far from a stroke of genius.

BECAUSE OF OUR tendency to see surprises on the periphery as outliers, it is important that you keep a notepad accessible near your bed or everywhere you go that you can use to take notes when unexpected ideas strike. You'll be surprised at how effective some of your ideas can be.

The next time you are straining to think up a solution for a creative project, step away from it and engage in mind-drifting activities to let ideas flow in.

It is worth knowing that experiencing an aha moment elicits exuberance. Surprisingly, we are not as happy when we solve a problem using our analytical skills—no matter how complex the problem is.[17]

When Meditation Kills Creativity

Traditional meditation requires that you focus on a certain object, your breath, a candle, etc. When your mind wanders, you are to beware of it and slowly bring your attention back to the object of focus. The goal is to stay in the present moment and not let your mind wander. Over time, this process strengthens your prefrontal cortex, which helps you attain stronger self-control and attention while at the same time reducing mind wandering.

As we covered before, intense focus on the task at hand inhibits your creative juice. While meditation creates a positive outcome for focus enhancement, it does the opposite in inducing creativity. Mind wandering flexes your idea-generator muscle. It is also the reason that people with attention deficit hyperactivity disorder score high in creativity.[18]

Creative work requires both focus inside and the ability to explore the outside. The traditional focused-attention meditation addresses the focus-enhancement part but weakens external exploration by reducing the occurrence of mind wandering.

Practicing a meditation that emphasizes subjective experience instead of a particular point of focus seems to provide greater improvement in creativity.[19] Transcendental Meditation, open-monitoring meditation, and relaxation response meditation techniques accept mind wandering as part of the process. They focus on subjective experiences instead of correcting thoughts or behavior. The meditators do not judge their wandering mind. It is a welcomed process in the practice. Your mind is encouraged to flow freely, which enables access to your subconscious memories and thus helps to generate ideas.[20] In this type of meditation, you notice your wandering mind and gradually bring it back to the object of focus. Taking this step helps you raise your capacity to switch between your mind's creative side and analytical side.

Focused-Attention and Open-Monitoring Meditation

The ability to shift between mentally wandering and concentrating on a creative project sets the stage for successful creative work. This is essential not only for creativity but also for the healthy development of your cognitive control.[21] Research shows that people who have practiced this type of open-monitoring meditation are better able to solve problems with multiple right answers compared to those who practiced traditional, focused-based meditation, who are better at solving problems with a single right answer.[22]

DON'T DISREGARD ideas even if they sound foolish. Creative ideas are usually generated at an unexpected moment. In that same vein, we tend to dismiss creative ideas as oddballs—or even outright ridiculous—as they come to our minds because we never expect them to solve the problem we have. Unintentional solutions work surprisingly well, just like falling in love.

7

THE LIFE'S WORK

> Those who actively create and re-create themselves are truly free spirits—artistic creators of their own lives.
>
> — FRIEDRICH NIETZSCHE

As children, we weren't afraid to dream. We dreamed often and were convinced we could achieve all our goals one day. As we aged, we came to realize that becoming an astronaut was not just about enjoying floating out in space, that becoming a doctor was not just about getting the chance to help sick children, or that being a firefighter was not about chasing after fireballs. We may have realized we didn't actually want those dreams anymore.

Adult life is not as free as we thought. Yes, we were free to sleep late, watch TV shows whenever we wanted, or buy video games with our own money. But we may also be enslaved to our job just so we could pay our bills and debts. We may have built a luxurious lifestyle, but quitting our job would put it in jeopardy. Life did not turn out as rosy as we envisioned it to be as a child. Confronted by the harsh reality that life is not smooth sailing, we strive to find the highest-paying job—even if the work does not align with our desire.

Our dream is crippled by the desire to make more money as we see reality fail to live up to our expectations. Our dreams were confounded over time by what we thought would make us *look* successful. We ceased to be interested in the things we were born to do.

Being a skilled orator, Dr. Martin Luther King Jr. was selected by his church members to bring an end to the segregation of the black and white races in the state of Alabama. Despite the dangerous road ahead, King chose to devote his life to helping others. He would become an integral part of the civil rights movement. The trials and tribulations that King faced throughout his lifetime fueled the fire that burned in his eyes every time he spoke.

If you were invincible, had an unlimited amount of money, and any work you did would guarantee success, what would you do? Perhaps you would want to travel around the world, buy the biggest house, and indulge in the best gourmet food. After satisfying all those *wants* and *cravings*, what would you do? Think about it. This question forces you to look deep inside and rethink who you really are in life by disregarding your present limitations. Perhaps you want to obliterate the world's illiteracy by placing library kiosks around the world or invent a new technology to help the elderly, or build a virtual school with 3D holographic teachers.

Realistically, your dream must match your gift. It must also be one that you fall in love with so that you are willing to devote the rest of your life to it. It must be one that you are happy to dedicate decades of effort to deal with the difficult, boring, exhausting, monotonous process of actualizing it. Dreaming is not enough; you must also put in the hard work.

The Work You Were Born to Do

Use your gift as the compass to determine your life's work. Most successful people use their gifts to speed up their success by doing what they do best. It is not a coincidence that they have a career that they love. They love what they do, and they are good at it.

Do you have fighter-pilot blood coursing through your veins but have never enrolled in flight training because your parents said becoming a lawyer would be a better fit for you?

Are you skillful at writing songs but have never tried to produce a single because you are too busy working at your high-paying corporate job?

Do you live and breathe fashion but have never designed a single article of clothing because your desk-bound job pays better?

Work on the task that is most relevant to your personal goals. Use your gift to answer the call of your destiny. What makes you truly alive is the opportunity to do what you do best with your gift. Doing that fine work you are born to do. Performing an act that is an extension of yourself. Actualizing the dream you fell in love with. Finding meaning in the universe through what you create. This will bridge your inner world with the outside world and make you feel complete.

Imagine this: At a tender age, you were good at playing chess. You remembered checkmating some adults. But your parents did not nurture that skill of yours. They got you to study hard to get into medical school. You hated dealing with medical terms, but you had no choice. After graduating from medical school, you applied for a job at a hospital. You were squeamish, despised going into the surgical theater, and dragged yourself to work every day. But life was good. You earned a good paycheck to support your family.

Would you be a chess grandmaster had you pursued a chess career? Probably. There is no guarantee of success in life. But, by forgoing your innate ability, you missed the chance to show the world the best version of yourself that you could be. The recognition you yearn for was denied to you.

As you proceed with doing what you must do, you unshackle yourself from your inner conflict and bring out that powerful desire to achieve the ideal version of yourself.[1] Use your gift to answer the call of your destiny.

ABRAHAM MASLOW's hierarchy of needs shows that self-actualization can only be attempted once we fulfill the rest of the needs beneath it. It is a commonly acceptable tenet because most people only look forward to developing their full potential after satiating the rest of their needs.

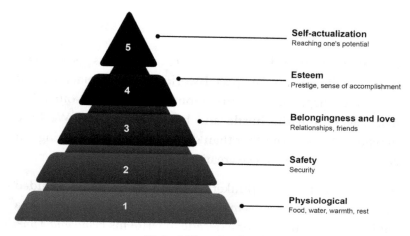

Maslow's Hierarchy of Needs

But one need not be constrained by this theory.

- You can write a groundbreaking poem even if you have not satisfied your psychological needs for prestige.
- You can surrender your safety needs and the physiological discomfort of going into a war zone to help children.
- You can deprive yourself of intimate relationships and friends temporarily to set your focus on completing that literary masterpiece.

Start your life's work whenever your circumstances permit. A fulfilling life doesn't hinge on attaining esteem beforehand.

Lonely Intellects

> One can be instructed in society, one is inspired only in solitude.

— JOHANN WOLFGANG VON GOETHE

Engaging exclusively in solitude, which is seemingly unproductive in this fast-paced world, is the primary way of liberating imagination. In that moment of solitude, our mind disengages from the hustle and bustle of city life. We have nowhere else to turn other than our own thoughts, making it a conducive time to produce creative work.

Some eminent creative thinkers deliberately lived in a secluded place to create their opus magnum. Martin Heidegger lived in a cabin near a mountain for a decade to write his *Being and Time*. Henry David Thoreau resided in a small cabin in Massachusetts, where he wrote some of the greatest American literature of the nineteenth century. Marcel Proust, a French novelist, wrote his 3,000-page masterpiece, *Remembrance of Things Past*, behind a closed door in his bedroom in Boulevard Haussmann.

Solitude is not to be confused with escaping reality. It is confronting reality.[2] Only in silence can we look straight into our inner landscape of thoughts, observe the spectrum of our emotions, listen to the world around us, examine the unexamined aspects of ourselves, develop our inner wisdom, and discover our true selves.

Creative work is a lonely endeavor. It is best done alone. Just the artist and the work. In solitude, ideas are crystallized. The artist is free to express himself to the fullest capacity with no extrinsic influence or intervention. Solitude forces the artist to slow down, dive deep into his own imagination, forge his unique perspective, and feed his creative mind.

In the presence of others, we tend to short-change our ideas. We fear that many of our notions may sound foolish to others, making us reluctant to showcase any idea at all.[3]

Time alone is not a luxury, despite what our modern society may believe. It is a mandatory step toward great creativity. This is not only applicable to artists but also to business leaders and all human beings seeking to produce their life's work.

Inevitable Rejection

 The world in general disapproves of creativity.

— ISAAC ASIMOV

Pursuing one's life's work does not always come easy. Creating an original work that is truly yours may bring about some degrees of resistance from others. You may end up contemplating sacrificing your originality to satisfy the masses.

No matter how much people say they revel in creativity, deep inside, people dislike creative solutions. A creative solution is unorthodox, non-conforming, and unconventional, and it defies whatever normal practice has always worked well in its stead. Creative solutions generate uncertainty, which feels uncomfortable and potentially threatening.

The level of a creative contribution is correlated to how much the work deviates from the mass's norm.[4] History has brought us many cases of rejected work that eventually took the world by storm.

- Lady Gaga's eccentric costumes and music were heavily criticized.
- Apple's decision to discontinue the OpenDoc framework was met with friction.

- Jazz music was condemned for a century before it was recognized as one of America's greatest contributions to music.
- Joseph Heller's unconventional World War II novel, *Catch-22*, was rejected until it finally became widely read and acknowledged as one of the best novels of its era.
- Even teachers in general dislike creative students.[5]

Producing one's life's work takes courage and the boldness to confront rejection until the work becomes mainstream and sets the course for the new standard. Human civilization can be propelled forward by confronting the status quo with novel work.

Fear of rejection, failure, and isolation stops many people from pursuing their life's work. Embrace the rejection for we are breaking the popular ways of thinking to establish fresh solutions. Rejection is the price one must be prepared to pay in pursuing one's life's work.

Bet More

Your life's work, no matter how invested you are in it, does not guarantee success. As a matter of fact, there is no one creative genius in the world who can consistently produce groundbreaking work.[6]

- Beethoven, touted as the greatest composer of all time, composed some mediocre symphonies too.[7]
- The tech mogul Steve Jobs failed many more times than he succeeded.
- After Shakespeare's famous *Hamlet*, he produced some plays that failed to live up to his fame.

- An average of approximately one-third of Thomas Edison's invention patents were approved. Of the 1,093 approved patents, only a handful became hits.[8]
- J.K. Rowling's bestseller *Harry Potter* was rejected by twelve publishers. The one who finally accepted it did so simply because the owner's daughter liked the book.

With persistence and by placing multiple bets on your life's task, you will increase your chances of creating a masterpiece.[9] Be bold and unconventional. Be prepared for the possibility that your work may fail.

WHEN FORTUNE SMILES upon one of your bets, people are likely to look up to you as an expert in that field, that your idea was a stroke of genius. The truth is, you might have learned from iterations of trials and attempts and from multiple bets. One bet's failure offers insight to learn and place a better, subsequent bet.

Pablo Picasso created over 50,000 works of art before his stark and shocking *Guernica* painting took off. Ninety percent of Apple's products have been failures. Rovio Entertainment developed 51 games before its *Angry Birds* skyrocketed the company's value to $1 billion. In one's quest to win over our unpredictable world, it pays to cast your net wider. You never know which idea might be accepted by the market. Some companies learn to exploit the opportunities of spreading their bets; for example, employees at Google are given budgets and time to work on new inventions.

Spreading your bets comes with an ultimate limitation: your resources. If you have limited resources, you can't deploy many projects. And when the project you complete fails in the market, you tend to be turned off from pursuing further projects.

It is thus important that you not exhaust your resources on a single project. Contrary to popular belief, investing more resources into a project does not increase its likelihood of success. Apple's $500 million project, Newton, was out-competed by a $3 million project, Palm Pilot, by Palm Computing. Apple has sufficient funding to secure top-tier talent and buy state-of-the-art devices, and yet everything still fell short when compared to its rival's low-cost project. Therefore, you and I have the same chance to succeed, even without as many resources.

Going all out for a project is beneficial if you can get it right the first time, which is rarely the case. By keeping some wherewithal available to fund subsequent projects, you can launch more bets to increase your chance of success.

It is important that you bet on your life's work with the following in mind:

1. Pick the work that intrigues you the most.

Psychologically, it is not nearly as easy to learn and retry when your money is at stake. When the failure rate of your bets has been steady for a long time, your desire to continue with subsequent bets can dissipate to the point that you quit prematurely.

You want to marry your life's work to your gift. Your interest in the work is a powerful catalyst for getting past the inevitable fiascos that will occur. Your desire to get your bet right will keep you unfazed and unfettered in the face of challenges.

2. Assess how much you are willing to lose.

WE ARE MOSTLY CONDITIONED to view a project's potential by how much revenue it can bring back. With the unpredictability of the market, ROI is not a good metric. No one can predict a start-up that can turn unicorn or a painting that can turn into a masterpiece. Furthermore, forecasting potential revenue can lead us into the trap of betting with a colossal budget, which can blow up our ability and drive to run the next bet.

Instead of focusing on potential gains, calibrate your life's work by taking into account losses that you can afford. When you are comfortable with a small loss, you can quickly recover to place your next bet.

3. Spot the opportunity.

PFIZER INTENDED to fabricate a drug to treat angina (chest pain), but its side effects led them to produce Viagra instead. North of Sweden, Yngve Bergqvist built an igloo art gallery out of ice and snow to attract tourists to the area. But after some of them asked to stay for the night, he turned it into Icehotel, and it became one of the most iconic tourist destinations in the country.

After you place a bet, you may receive a totally unexpected outcome. Most of us would dismiss this outcome as irrelevant and move on. However, such an unexpected result might present a new opportunity. Remember that aha moments are always unexpected.

4. Create the ripple effect.

No bet you produce starts from zero. Your bets get better after each iteration thanks to accumulating insights on what works and what does not. The more you export ideas out into the world, the more you are subjected to the randomness of new events that may set you in motion. Your previous bets become proof of your reputation, which increases with every subsequent one.

Michelle Phan had been uploading makeup tutorials to YouTube. When Lady Gaga's fans discovered her tutorial, "How to Get Lady Gaga's Eyes," her video went viral. At the same time, the rest of her videos got discovered too, snowballing her career and the YouTuber's subscriber's growth.

5. Double down your wager on a working bet.

In the beginning, when you are unsure of which project to work on with your skills, go wide with your bets. When you find one that starts to gain traction, channel more resources into it to propel its success. The drawback is that you will be required to kill most (if not all) of your other projects to re-invest your resources into that single one.

Because of the popularity of the video game *Angry Birds*, Rovio went all out in producing merchandise, T-shirts, books, and more. Gain momentum and capitalize on the success wave.

Give Your Work Away

 Life's most persistent and urgent question is, 'What are you doing for others?'

— DR. MARTIN LUTHER KING, JR.

Produce your life's work to enhance the lives of others, parlay a seedbed for a future breakthrough, or liberate the populace from oppression. Starting your life's work is the best thing you could ever do for yourself. The world needs you to be yourself, not an imitation of someone else's work.

Once you have found your life's work, the biggest question remains, "*Why must you give it away?*" Shouldn't you hog the fruition of your life's work for your own benefit? Everything that is a vital part of our collective lifestyle today, such as advanced technologies, modern-day transport, sanitary healthcare facilities, and countless others, all exist because of the hard work of our ancestors. With all the benefits we have enjoyed, it's only right to contribute to posterity.

- If you are a teacher, strive to transform the lives of your students.
- If you are a reporter, go all out to share your knowledge with the world.
- If you are a politician, be an icon who is there for the people, not for power.
- If you are a cook, create delectable dishes and delight people.

One of the premier indicators of achievement and well-being is having the ability to pair what you are doing with enhancing other people's lives. Acts of generosity allow oxytocin to be released in your brain, which, in turn, causes you to be happy. The happiness cascades and flourishes in your life's work. With that extra jolt of energy, you shift into a higher gear to produce more, contribute more, and touch more people. Finally, there is something in you that can make someone's life better for good. What a wonderful feeling.

If the work you do makes you happy, imagine the profound effect it will have on your well-being every day. You will *live* more than most people would in several lifetimes. You will experience a greater sense of belonging. You will stay positive and lead a fulfilling life full of meaning and purpose.

Ask yourself, *"How many people would be positively influenced by what I can do?"* Then, follow up with that question by asking, *"How many more will benefit long after I am gone?"*

Ponder those questions and decide on the contributions your work can offer to elevate others or improve others' lives. Aim to make a contribution that will grow infinitely. Share your gift with the world.

At work, we are often so caught up in our job's routine that we fail to notice the contribution we can make for others. There is always an opportunity to serve others—even in a monotonous vocation.

Do your job with the purpose to serve in mind. Put a smile on others' faces. Make their lives easier. Instead of just going to work for the paycheck, look at how your work can improve others' lives.

Above all, our life is transitory. Don't leave the world empty-handed. Make your most substantive contribution over your lifetime. You will not come out of life alive, but your life's work will.

When Your Job Inhibits Contributions

We all want our contributions to count, even if it's only in a tiny way. Unfortunately, we sometimes get demotivated to pursue any greater contributions than our job description necessitates. That seems to be mostly caused by our desire to hold onto our own things. Despite this, we also know how fulfilling it is to contribute to our colleagues. A person who enjoys educating her layman customers so that she can save them hours of manual labor is highly gratified. Creating an excellent meal that puts diners in a good mood is extremely satisfying for a chef.

Most businesses hire employees for the service their employees will provide. You're paid to do this and that; therefore, you just do it. Your personal development is not part of your job description. Business profits come first before your well-being. There is a lack of autonomy, trust, and support. You do the job because you have to, not because you want to.

On the one hand, colleagues and associates can be self-serving. Such a situation is indicated when:

- Your contribution is taken for granted
- Your goodwill is treated as an obligation
- Your boss hogs all the credit
- Your manager demands that you work longer hours

Confronted with such a situation, there's no way anyone can turn their job into their life's work—even if the job equals your passion. There is no way anyone wants to connect an unhealthy work environment with the positive influence the job has on something bigger than himself. Contributing more would be career suicide and create more baggage than we can handle. We thus stop our charity work and hop jobs, hoping to find that dream job that allows us to do just what we are good at.

Toxic jobs harm our souls rather than enhance them and potentially shorten our lives over time. A body of research shows that an unemployed person fares better overall than a person stuck in a toxic job.[10] If you are an employee, realize that you can't expect a utopian environment in every workplace you find. No one can (or should) rely on companies to change their system to make it fertile ground in which to develop your life's work.

Join a company that enables you to do your life's work, allows you to put your talents to work, values its staff, offers a job that serves your life, and enables you to work healthily. While not always easy to find, it will pay a lot of dividends to look for a position that will allow you to work meaningfully. You will do your work better and enjoy it more.

The Turning Point

 I paint in order not to cry.

— PAUL KLEE

After a negative experience, our mind challenges our old beliefs as they no longer hold up to the event. We struggle to make sense of what has unfolded before us. With the dismantling of our own assumptions and thought patterns, we awaken new perspectives as a coping mechanism. We enter a period of rebuilding ourselves to gain a new life.

Intense suffering can make us rethink our priorities, reconsider our hidebound opinions, and reevaluate long-standing convictions. It opens the mind up for exploration beyond a person's present strict and narrow point of view.[11] You retreat to your instinct to *live*; that is, to pursue your life's work. Having experienced suffering, you become more likely to contribute to humanity and act for the good of others.[12] Sometimes tragedy and inspiration go hand in hand.

Research has found some intriguing statistics regarding famous artists. Some of the greatest artists accomplished noteworthy life work after experiencing a life-threatening illness, debilitating accidents, or extreme grief.[13] They turned to works of art to divert their attention away from the traumatic events, heal psychologically, and find meaning in the suffering. They experienced a deeply profound improvement and let the work elevate their suffering.[14] While suffering from a rapid loss of hearing, Ludwig van Beethoven composed *Missa Solemnis*, one of his greatest works.

People who do not thrive off of such misery are often driven into a deep depression. What doesn't kill you physically can still kill you mentally. On the other hand, some who survive tragedies experience some positive psychological growth and emerge with a new appreciation for life that they can parlay into a feverish desire to complete their life's work.[15] Van Gogh, who struggled with deep anxiety, sent himself to Saint-Rémy-de-Provence prison and created the iconic *Starry Night*. While suffering from an autoimmune disease that disabled his hands in 1936, Paul Klee painted more than 264 pictures in 1937, 489 in 1938, and 1,254 in 1939.[16] The works of Francisco de Goya after he experienced health challenges are among his best.[17]

Many highly skilled individuals also experience parental loss.[18] Among the most famous are Abraham Lincoln, Charles Darwin, and Ludwig van Beethoven. Parental loss also leads to feelings of vulnerability in youngsters. They do not have any alternative but to rely on their talents. That response can create a massive focus on developing their abilities throughout their childhood and into adulthood to restore the sense of security that had been shaken.

In contrast, if life is too easy, our intuition prefers to conserve energy. There is less motivation and reason to work hard. If Brazilian kids had access to luxurious toys, they might be less driven to practice soccer extensively. The unusually high percentage of top-level soccer players is the result of both nature and nurture.

That said, there is no need to seek out tragedy to unleash your greatest potential. Though tragedy can be a great catalyst for change and inspiration, negative circumstances can ultimately claim your life, leaving you unable to explore any last-minute epiphany and take action.

Research shows that a very positive experience could trigger a revelation too.[19] Examples of such positive experiences include:

- Meeting an inspiring person
- Reading a book that challenges the way you think
- Connecting to something greater than oneself
- Producing work that leads to new opportunities
- Taking up a new routine that changes your life
- Exposing yourself to an experience that opens up new possibilities in your life

Good vibes often beget more good vibes. It takes willpower to push yourself beyond procrastination. The second book of the series, *Peak Self-Control*, provides a comprehensive guide to optimizing your willpower.

All of us are just a collection of cells in the vast universe. We are born, make a dent in the world, and then die. Rinse and repeat. Some make the world better; some make it worse. We yearn for meaning to our existence. It feels empty when the work we do means nothing to our life. Each of us was bestowed a precious gift for life. With that gift comes a purpose for which our inherent meaning emerges.

You are part of the solution. You have something to give, and you have people who need it. Make this world a better place than it was when you came into it. You are at an exciting moment in history. Never before have there been so many opportunities available to us. The world is waiting for your contribution.

WITH THAT, we reach the last chapter of this book. I hope you will begin to appreciate the dimensional beauty of finding your gift and then give it away through your life's work.

CONCLUSION

Remember that all your possessions, fame, and wealth are temporary in life. There is more to life than focusing too much on earning those.

Use your remaining time on earth to hone your gift, maximize your potential, and do something for posterity. Make each day a discovery of what you can be. Accomplishing dreams you care about through creative achievement and fulfillment gives meaning to your existence. The day you stop having something to look forward to is the day you have lost hope.

Make it a habit to break a routine. Deliberately dive back into an unfamiliar experience once in a while to stimulate your brain's creative muscles and increase your odds of encountering an aha moment.

Pursuing one's life's work is an arduous journey, but with the right tools and mindset, anything is possible. When we can no longer change the fluidity of the unpredictable world, we are bound to change ourselves.

You have control over your destiny, no matter what others have said about you. It is never too late to start cultivating your latent potential. The only thing that shall stop you from pursuing your goal is yourself. You are the only one who can set your limits. You are the only one who can stop yourself from trying, learning, and developing.

If you have not reached your full potential, I can tell you this much—it is not because you are not good or talented enough. It is because you have not put in the hard work required to get the results you want. As Nietzsche put it, "He who has a *why* to live for can bear almost any *how*."

Thanks for reading this book.

KEEP IN TOUCH

There is no better satisfaction for an author than seeing readers get a glow from reading his books. If this book benefits you, leave me a review, will you? I haven't grown tired of reading reviews from people who have reaped benefits from this series. Reading their reviews makes me feel utterly satisfied and can bring tears to my eyes.

Keep in touch with me at said@saidhasyim.com.

If you wish to be notified of my next book update or special promotion, sign up to my mailing list at https://www.saidhasyim.com.

For a limited time and while stocks last, access the bonus material at https://www.saidhasyim.com/peak-life-s-work-exclusive if you purchased this book.

ALSO BY SAID HASYIM

ABOUT THE AUTHOR

 Said Hasyim is the founder of BookSentry with an obsession for finding the best ways to maximize his productivity. After more than a decade of arduous self-experimentation and research into bio-hacks, Said discovered various methods to improve his productivity. Now, he hopes to share his findings with his readers in his *Peak Productivity* book series to unleash their inner potential.

Find out more about Said at www.saidhasyim.com.

facebook.com/SaidHasyimReal

instagram.com/SaidHasyimReal

linkedin.com/in/saidhasyim

NOTES

1. The Gift

1. Oliver, C., Oxener, G., Hearn, M. & Hall, S. (2001). Effects of social proximity on multiple aggressive behaviors. *Journal of Applied Behavior Analysis*, *34*(1), 85—88. https://doi.org/10.1901/jaba.2001.34-85.

2. Character Strengths

1. Ruch, W. & Proyer, R. T. (2015). Mapping strengths into virtues: the relation of the 24 VIA-strengths to six ubiquitous virtues. *Frontiers in Psychology*, *6*, 460. https://doi.org/10.3389/fpsyg.2015.00460.
2. Hudson, N. W. & Fraley, R. C. (2015). Volitional personality trait change: Can people choose to change their personality traits? *Journal of Personality and Social Psychology*, *109*(3), 490—507. https://doi.org/10.1037/pspp0000021.
3. Martínez-Martí, M. L. & Ruch, W. (2014). Character strengths and well-being across the life span: data from a representative sample of German-speaking adults living in Switzerland. *Frontiers in Psychology*, *5*, 1253. https://doi.org/10.3389/fpsyg.2014.01253.
4. Knight Z. G. (2017). A proposed model of psychodynamic psychotherapy linked to Erik Erikson's eight stages of psychosocial development. *Clinical Psychology & Psychotherapy*, *24*(5), 1047–1058. https://doi.org/10.1002/cpp.2066.
5. Swartz, T. H., Palermo, A. S., Masur, S. K., & Aberg, J. A. (2019). The Science and Value of Diversity: Closing the Gaps in Our Understanding of Inclusion and Diversity. *The Journal of Infectious Diseases*, *220*(220 Suppl 2), S33—S41. https://doi.org/10.1093/infdis/jiz174.

3. Skill

1. Wong, N. C. (2015). The 10 000-hour rule. *Canadian Urological Association Journal*, *9*(9—10), 299.
2. Macnamara, B. N. & Maitra, M. (2019). The role of deliberate practice in expert performance: revisiting Ericsson, Krampe & Tesch-Römer (1993). *Royal Society Open Science*, *6*(8), 190327. https://doi.org/10.1098/rsos.190327.

3. Macnamara, B. N., Hambrick, D. Z. & Oswald, F. L. (2014). Deliberate practice and performance in music, games, sports, education, and professions: a meta-analysis. *Psychological science*, 25(8), 1608—1618. https://doi.org/10.1177/0956797614535810.

4. Wikipedia contributors. (2022, June 10). *Susan Polgar*. Wikipedia. Retrieved August 26, 2022, from https://en.wikipedia.org/wiki/Susan_Polgar.

5. Simonton, D. K. (2012). Taking the U.S. Patent Office Criteria Seriously: A Quantitative Three-Criterion Creativity Definition and Its Implications. *Creativity Research Journal*, 24(2—3), 97—106. https://doi.org/10.1080/10400419.2012.676974.

6. Frensch, P. A. & Sternberg, R. J. (1989). Expertise and intelligent thinking: When is it worse to know better? In R. J. Sternberg (Ed.), *Advances in the Psychology of Human Intelligence*, Vol. 5, pp. 157—188). Lawrence Erlbaum Associates, Inc.

7. Simonton, D. K. (1994). *Greatness: Who Makes History and Why* (1st ed.). The Guilford Press.

8. Lippens, S., D'Enfert, C., Farkas, L., Kehres, A., Korn, B., Morales, M., Pepperkok, R., Premvardhan, L., Schlapbach, R., Tiran, A., Meder, D. & Van Minnebruggen, G. (2019). One step ahead: Innovation in core facilities. *EMBO Reports*, 20(4), e48017. https://doi.org/10.15252/embr.201948017.

9. Montani, L. & Suter, U. (2018). Building lipids for myelin. *Aging*, 10(5), 861—862. https://doi.org/10.18632/aging.101458.

10. Sheridan, H. & Reingold, E. M. (2014). Expert vs. novice differences in the detection of relevant information during a chess game: evidence from eye movements. *Frontiers in Psychology*, 5, 941. https://doi.org/10.3389/fpsyg.2014.00941.

11. Roseberry, S., Hirsh-Pasek, K., Parish-Morris, J. & Golinkoff, R. M. (2009). Live action: can young children learn verbs from video? *Child Development*, 80(5), 1360—1375.

12. Schwarz, J. (2007, August 7). *Baby DVDs, videos may hinder, not help, infants' language development*. UW News. Retrieved August 27, 2022, from https://www.washington.edu/news/2007/08/07/baby-dvds-videos-may-hinder-not-help-infants-language-development.

13. Adolph, K. E., Hoch, J. E. & Cole, W. G. (2018). Development (of Walking): 15 Suggestions. *Trends in Cognitive Sciences*, 22(8), 699–711. https://doi.org/10.1016/j.tics.2018.05.010.

14. Jaarsveld, S. & Lachmann, T. (2017). Intelligence and Creativity in Problem Solving: The Importance of Test Features in Cognition Research. *Frontiers in Psychology*, 8, 134. https://doi.org/10.3389/fpsyg.2017.00134.

15. *Study Challenges Theory About Left Brain/Right Brain Behavior*. (2013, August 15). WebMD. Retrieved August 27, 2022, from https://www.web-

md.com/mental-health/news/20130815/study-challenges-theory-about-left-brainright-brain-behavior.

16. Rosen, D. S., Oh, Y., Erickson, B., Zhang, F. Z., Kim, Y. E. & Kounios, J. (2020). Dual-process contributions to creativity in jazz improvisations: An SPM-EEG study. *NeuroImage*, *213*, 116632. https://doi.org/10.1016/j.neuroimage.2020.116632.

17. Tamana, S. K. et al. (2019). Screen-time is associated with inattention problems in preschoolers: Results from the CHILD birth cohort study. *PLOS One*, *14*(4), e0213995. https://doi.org/10.1371/journal.pone.0213995.

18. Stojanoski, B., Wild, C. J., Battista, M. E., Nichols, E. S. & Owen, A. M. (2021). Brain training habits are not associated with generalized benefits to cognition: An online study of over 1000 "brain trainers". *Journal of Experimental Psychology: General*, *150*(4), 729—738. https://doi.org/10.1037/xge0000773.

19. Macdonald, K., Germine, L., Anderson, A., Christodoulou, J. & McGrath, L. M. (2017). Dispelling the Myth: Training in Education or Neuroscience Decreases but Does Not Eliminate Beliefs in Neuromyths. *Frontiers in Psychology*, *8*. https://doi.org/10.3389/fpsyg.2017.01314.

20. Liederman, J. (1998). The Dynamics of Interhemispheric Collaboration and Hemispheric Control. *Brain and Cognition*, *36*(2), 193–208. https://doi.org/10.1006/brcg.1997.0952.

21. Paul, E. S. & Kaufman, S. B. (Eds.). (2014b). The Philosophy of Creativity. *Oxford Academic*. https://doi.org/10.1093/acprof:oso/9780199836963.001.0001.

22. Andreasen N. C. (2011). A journey into chaos: creativity and the unconscious. *Mens Sana Monographs*, *9*(1), 42—53.

4. Interest

1. Singha, S., Warr, M., Mishra, P. & Henriksen, D. (2020). Playing with Creativity Across the Lifespan: a Conversation with Dr. Sandra Russ. *TechTrends*, *64*(4), 550—554. https://doi.org/10.1007/s11528-020-00514-3.

2. Frost, J. L. (2009). *A History of Children's Play and Play Environments: Toward a Contemporary Child-Saving Movement* (1st ed.). Routledge.

3. Wang, S. & Aamodt, S. (2012). *Play, stress, and the learning brain*. Cerebrum: the Dana forum on brain science, 2012, 12.

4. Suggate, S. P., Schaughency, E. A. & Reese, E. (2013). Children learning to read later catch up to children reading earlier. *Early Childhood Research Quarterly*, *28*(1), 33–48. https://doi.org/10.1016/j.ecresq.2012.04.004.

5. Berretta, S. & Privette, G. (1990). Influence of play on creative thinking. *Perceptual and Motor Skills*, *71*(2), 659–666. https://doi.org/10.2466/pms.1990.71.2.659.

6. Lee, E. Y., Bains, A., Hunter, S., Ament, A., Brazo-Sayavera, J., Carson, V., Hakimi, S., Huang, W. Y., Janssen, I., Lee, M., Lim, H., Silva, D. & Tremblay, M. S. (2021). Systematic review of the correlates of outdoor play and time among children aged 3-12 years. *The International Journal of Behavioral Nutrition and Physical Activity*, *18*(1), 41. https://doi.org/10.1186/s12966-021-01097-9.

5. Talent

1. Karpen S. C. (2018). The Social Psychology of Biased Self-Assessment. *American Journal of Pharmaceutical Education*, *82*(5), 6299. https://doi.org/10.5688/ajpe6299.
2. Wikipedia contributors. (2022b, August 1). *Football in Brazil*. Wikipedia. Retrieved August 27, 2022, from https://en.wikipedia.org/wiki/Football_in_Brazil.
3. Uehara, L., Falcous, M., Button, C., Davids, K., Araújo, D., de Paula, A. R. & Saunders, J. (2021). The Poor "Wealth" of Brazilian Football: How Poverty May Shape Skill and Expertise of Players. *Frontiers in Sports and Active Living*, *3*. https://doi.org/10.3389/fspor.2021.635241.

6. Synergize the Gift

1. Icekson, T., Roskes, M., & Moran, S. (2014). Effects of optimism on creativity under approach and avoidance motivation. *Frontiers in Human Neuroscience*, *8*, 105. https://doi.org/10.3389/fnhum.2014.00105.
2. Beaty, R. E., Benedek, M., Silvia, P. J. & Schacter, D. L. (2016). Creative Cognition and Brain Network Dynamics. *Trends in Cognitive Sciences*, *20*(2), 87–95. https://doi.org/10.1016/j.tics.2015.10.004.
3. Jung-Beeman, M., Bowden, E. M., Haberman, J., Frymiare, J. L., Arambel-Liu, S., Greenblatt, R., Reber, P. J. & Kounios, J. (2004). Neural activity when people solve verbal problems with insight. *PLOS Biology*, *2*(4), E97. https://doi.org/10.1371/journal.pbio.0020097.
4. Kuldas, S., Ismail, H. N., Hashim, S. & Bakar, Z. A. (2013). Unconscious learning processes: mental integration of verbal and pictorial instructional materials. *SpringerPlus*, *2*(1), 105. https://doi.org/10.1186/2193-1801-2-105.
5. Lewicki, P., Hill, T. & Czyzewska, M. (1992). Nonconscious acquisition of information. *The American Psychologist*, *47*(6), 796—801. https://doi.org/10.1037//0003-066x.47.6.796.
6. Wikipedia contributors. (2021, May 10). *Philosopher's Walk*. Wikipedia. Retrieved August 27, 2022, from https://en.wikipedia.org/wiki/Philosopher%27s_Walk.

7. Oppezzo, M., & Schwartz, D. L. (2014). Give your ideas some legs: The positive effect of walking on creative thinking. *Journal of Experimental Psychology: Learning, Memory, and Cognition, 40*(4), 1142—1152. https://doi.org/10.1037/a0036577.

8. Zedelius, C. M., Protzko, J., Broadway, J. M. & Schooler, J. W. (2021). What types of daydreaming predict creativity? Laboratory and experience sampling evidence. *Psychology of Aesthetics, Creativity, and the Arts, 15*(4), 596—611. https://doi.org/10.1037/aca0000342.

9. Smallwood, J., Schooler, J. W., Turk, D. J., Cunningham, S. J., Burns, P. & Macrae, C. N. (2011). Self-reflection and the temporal focus of the wandering mind. *Consciousness and Cognition, 20*(4), 1120—1126. https://doi.org/10.1016/j.concog.2010.12.017.

10. Hansgrohe study: *The brightest ideas begin in the shower.* (2015, January 26). 2015-01-26 | Plumbing and Mechanical | Plumbing & Mechanical. Retrieved August 27, 2022, from https://www.pmmag.com/articles/96968-hansgrohe-study-the-brightest-ideas-begin-in-the-shower.

11. Amabile, T. M., Hadley, C. N. & Kramer, S. J. (2002). Creativity under the gun. *Harvard Business Review, 80*(8), 52–147.

12. Tadmor, C. T., Galinsky, A. D. & Maddux, W. W. (2012). Getting the most out of living abroad: biculturalism and integrative complexity as key drivers of creative and professional success. *Journal of Personality and Social Psychology, 103*(3), 520—542. https://doi.org/10.1037/a0029360.

13. Neural Basis of Solving Problems with Insight. (2004). *PLOS Biology, 2*(4), e111. https://doi.org/10.1371/journal.pbio.0020111

14. Dunn, P. M. (2002). Stephane Tarnier (1828—1897), the architect of perinatology in France. *Archives of Disease in Childhood-Fetal and Neonatal Edition, 86*(2), 137F—139. https://doi.org/10.1136/fn.86.2.f137.

15. Simonton, D. K. (1997). Foreign influence and national achievement: The impact of open milieus on Japanese civilization. *Journal of Personality and Social Psychology, 72*(1), 86—94. https://doi.org/10.1037/0022-3514.72.1.86.

16. Ghiselin, B. (1963). Automatism, Intention, and Autonomy in the Novelist's Production. *Daedalus, 92*(2), 297—311. http://www.jstor.org/stable/20026779.

17. Oh, Y., Chesebrough, C., Erickson, B., Zhang, F., & Kounios, J. (2020). An insight-related neural reward signal. *NeuroImage, 214,* 116757. https://doi.org/10.1016/j.neuroimage.2020.116757

18. Boot, N., Nevicka, B. & Baas, M. (2020). Creativity in ADHD: Goal-Directed Motivation and Domain Specificity. *Journal of Attention Disorders, 24*(13), 1857—1866. https://doi.org/10.1177/1087054717727352.

19. Colzato, L. S., Ozturk, A. & Hommel, B. (2012). Meditate to create: the impact of focused-attention and open-monitoring training on convergent and divergent thinking. *Frontiers in Psychology, 3,* 116. https://doi.org/10.3389/fpsyg.2012.00116.

20. https://news.harvard.edu/gazette/story/2018/06/mindfulness-meditation-and-relaxation-response-affect-brain-differently.

21. Immordino-Yang, M. H., Christodoulou, J. A. & Singh, V. (2012). Rest Is Not Idleness: Implications of the Brain's Default Mode for Human Development and Education. *Perspectives on Psychological Science: a Journal of the Association for Psychological Science*, 7(4), 352—364. https://doi.org/10.1177/1745691612447308.

22. Colzato, L. S., Ozturk, A. & Hommel, B. (2012). Meditate to Create: The Impact of Focused-Attention and Open-Monitoring Training on Convergent and Divergent Thinking. *Frontiers in Psychology*, 3. https://doi.org/10.3389/fpsyg.2012.00116.

7. The Life's Work

1. Brennan, T. P. & Piechowski, M. M. (1991). A Developmental Framework for Self-Actualization. *Journal of Humanistic Psychology*, 31(3), 43—64. https://doi.org/10.1177/0022167891313008.

2. Naor, L. & Mayseless, O. (2020). The Wilderness Solo Experience: A Unique Practice of Silence and Solitude for Personal Growth. *Frontiers in Psychology*, 11. https://doi.org/10.3389/fpsyg.2020.547067.

3. *Why Capable People Are Reluctant to Lead*. (2020, December 17). Harvard Business Review. Retrieved August 27, 2022, from https://hbr.org/2020/12/why-capable-people-are-reluctant-to-lead.

4. *Psychology says that outsiders are the most innovative people.* (2016, January 20). Business Insider. Retrieved August 27, 2022, from https://www.businessinsider.com/why-outsiders-are-the-most-innovative-people-2016-1?international=true&r=US&IR=T.

5. Westby, E. L. & Dawson, V. (1995). Creativity: Asset or Burden in the Classroom? *Creativity Research Journal*, 8(1), 1–10. https://doi.org/10.1207/s15326934crj0801_1.

6. Kaufman, S. B., Christopher, E. M. & Kaufman, J. C. (2008). The Genius Portfolio: How Do Poets Earn Their Creative Reputations from Multiple Products? *Empirical Studies of the Arts*, 26(2), 181–196. https://doi.org/10.2190/em.26.2.c

7. Simonton, D. K. (2015). Numerical Odds and Evens in Beethoven's Nine Symphonies. *Empirical Studies of the Arts*, 33(1), 18—35. https://doi.org/10.1177/0276237415569980.

8. (n.d.). *Edison's Patents*. Rutgers School of Arts and Sciences. https://edison.rutgers.edu/life-of-edison/edison-s-patents.

9. Simonton, D. K. (2011). Creativity and Discovery as Blind Variation: Campbell's (1960) BVSR Model after the Half-Century Mark. *Review of General Psychology*, 15(2), 158—174. https://doi.org/10.1037/a0022912.

10. Chandola, T. & Zhang, N. (2017). Re-employment, job quality, health and allostatic load biomarkers: prospective evidence from the UK Household Longitudinal Study. *International Journal of Epidemiology*, 47(1), 47—57. https://doi.org/10.1093/ije/dyx150.

11. Wagner, A. C., Torbit, L., Jenzer, T., Landy, M. S., Pukay-Martin, N. D., Macdonald, A., Fredman, S. J. & Monson, C. M. (2016). The Role of Posttraumatic Growth in a Randomized Controlled Trial of Cognitive-Behavioral Conjoint Therapy for PTSD. *Journal of Traumatic Stress*, 29(4), 379—383. https://doi.org/10.1002/jts.22122.

12. Greenberg, D. M., Baron-Cohen, S., Rosenberg, N., Fonagy, P. & Rentfrow, P. J. (2018). Elevated empathy in adults following childhood trauma. *PLOS One*, 13(10), e0203886. https://doi.org/10.1371/journal.pone.0203886.

13. Ludwig, A. M. (1996). *The Price of Greatness: Resolving the Creativity and Madness Controversy*. The Guilford Press.

14. Ettun, R., Schultz, M. & Bar-Sela, G. (2014). Transforming Pain into Beauty: On Art, Healing, and Care for the Spirit. *Evidence-Based Complementary and Alternative Medicine*, 2014, 1—7. https://doi.org/10.1155/2014/789852.

15. Slade, M., Rennick-Egglestone, S., Blackie, L., Llewellyn-Beardsley, J., Franklin, D., Hui, A., Thornicroft, G., McGranahan, R., Pollock, K., Priebe, S., Ramsay, A., Roe, D. & Deakin, E. (2019). Post-traumatic growth in mental health recovery: qualitative study of narratives. *BMJ Open*, 9(6), e029342. https://doi.org/10.1136/bmjopen-2019-029342.

16. Wikipedia contributors. (2022c, August 21). *Paul Klee*. Wikipedia. Retrieved August 27, 2022, from https://en.wikipedia.org/wiki/Paul_Klee#Last_works_in_Switzerland.

17. Felisati, D., & Sperati, G. (2010). Francisco Goya and his illness. *Acta Otorhinolaryngologica Italica: organo ufficiale della Societa italiana di otorinolaringologia e chirurgia cervico-facciale, 30*(5), 264—270.

18. Albert, R. S. (1971). Cognitive Development and Parental Loss among the Gifted, the Exceptionally Gifted and the Creative. *Psychological Reports*, 29(1), 19—26. https://doi.org/10.2466/pro.1971.29.1.19.

19. Thrash, T. M., Maruskin, L. A., Cassidy, S. E., Fryer, J. W. & Ryan, R. M. (2010). Mediating between the muse and the masses: inspiration and the actualization of creative ideas. *Journal of Personality and Social Psychology*, 98(3), 469—487. https://doi.org/10.1037/a0017907.

CPSIA information can be obtained
at www.ICGtesting.com
Printed in the USA
BVHW052322271222
655118BV00007B/84